Our Tribe Chanting
A Spiritual Journeybook for Gay Men

The Companion Volume to
Two Flutes Playing
and
Two Hearts Dancing

Andrew Ramer

WITH A FOREWORD BY
Toby Johnson

RESOURCE *Publications* · Eugene, Oregon

OUR TRIBE CHANTING
A Spiritual Journeybook for Gay Men, The Companion Volume
to *Two Flutes Playing* and *Two Hearts Dancing*

Copyright © 2025 Andrew Ramer. All rights reserved. Except for brief quotations in critical publications or reviews, no part of this book may be reproduced in any manner without prior written permission from the publisher. Write: Permissions, Wipf and Stock Publishers, 199 W. 8th Ave., Suite 3, Eugene, OR 97401.

Resource Publications
An Imprint of Wipf and Stock Publishers
199 W. 8th Ave., Suite 3
Eugene, OR 97401

www.wipfandstock.com

PAPERBACK ISBN: 979-8-3852-3753-1
HARDCOVER ISBN: 979-8-3852-3754-8
EBOOK ISBN: 979-8-3852-3755-5

VERSION NUMBER 01/22/25

"The first book in his pioneering trilogy, *Two Flutes Playing*, helped us reclaim a sense of where we are as a queer people with a deep heritage and purpose. His second volume, *Two Hearts Dancing*, helped us fall in love with ourselves and each other. In *Our Tribe Chanting*, the rapturous conclusion of the trilogy, he passionately and tenderly takes each of us by the hand and guides us into who we are becoming. With warmth and humor, he reflects on his queer journey and invites us to reflect upon our own, even as he calls us to the most generous embodiment of our truths and the greatest embrace of our destiny: we are here, quite literally, to save the world."

—**Hunter Flournoy**, director, Spirit Journeys

"Be quick to take the hand of our cherished elder. We queer men have work to do, and Eli Andrew Ramer's teachings in this vibrant book will enthrone you in the chair of wisdom."

—**Will Roscoe**, author of *Queer Spirits: A Gay Men's Myth Book* and *Jesus and the Shamanic Tradition of Same-Sex Love*

"Every ethnic group has a mythology passed down from parent to child, but for many of us who are queer, rooting ourselves in the past has been, at best, a challenge. Until, that is, Eli Andrew Ramer. Ramer weaves together the dreams, visions, and magic of our people in a way that, finally, makes us whole. 'For us,' says Ramer, 'prayer is about the things we say.' *Our Tribe Chanting* gives voice to the countless generations of us who were, are, and will be."

—**Andrew Lawler**, author of *A Perfect Frenzy*

"The image that keeps popping into my head as I read *Our Tribe Chanting* is Virgil. Eli Andrew Ramer is our guide, our visionary, a seer. He invites us to see in new ways and walks us through the liminal moments all around us. He pulls back the curtain to reveal the magic and elevates us all."

—**Bo Young**, publisher of *Gay Wisdom*

"I recommend Eli's book *Our Tribe Chanting: A Spiritual Journeybook for Gay Men* with utter delight! Delight at the skillful and beautiful ways in which he weaves together myth, autobiography, spiritual wisdom, bodily sensuality, and queer being. At a time when many of us older queer folk are looking back on our lives, Eli's writing reminds us of—and recalls us to—a deeper way of living that brings us into ever closer connection with the larger tribe of queer souls who span time, place, and identity. Come join the chant!"

—**Bernie Schlager**, executive director, Center for LGBTQ and Gender Studies in Religion

"Before I discovered Eli Andrew Ramer my world was unendurably small. Now I take jaunts through countless universes and dimensions at a moment's notice. Now my world is as big as I am. A perfect fit. A mirror. A friend. And the most powerful reality-expander I know."

—**Randy Higgins**, author of *Salvo: Answers to an Apocalypse*

"Eli Ramer's message for gay men is radical, as in the Latin word for root: We have always been here, and are here for a purpose, each and all of us. These essays range from mytho-history to autobiography to valuable guidance on how to be—and how to be together. Generations have been moved and empowered by Ramer's previous books. *Our Tribe Chanting* will refresh and recenter that knowledge. Your first encounter? Prepare for change."

—**Jonathan Lerner**, author of *Performance Anxiety*

"Eli Andrew Ramer, a visionary historian, poet, prophet, storyteller, and teacher of sacred embodiment has guided and inspired the queer spirit community for over thirty years. This mischievous volume will delight, wherever we—youth or elder or anyone in between—are on our journey. The richness and depth of the essays are augmented with stimulating prompts expanding the fresh fun and spiritual sexiness. With its wit, warmth, and wisdom this uniquely eclectic offering by one of our veritable visionaries is truly a transformational agent."

—**Jim Van Buskirk**, editor of *There at the End: Voices from Final Exit Network*

"Eli Andrew Ramer's work speaks to the soul of what it means to be gay: we're part of a magical tribe of divine beings who have the privilege of operating in special functions that contribute to the healing and evolution of the world. Whether it's learning about the power of getting blessed by your gay elders, communing with the sanctuary of the forest, or reimagining the term 'fundamental,' *Our Tribe Chanting* will expand your consciousness toward greater pride and healing."

—**David Monticalvo**, author of *Celebrating Gay: Reclaiming Spirituality After a Lifetime of Shame*

"Eli Andrew Ramer is a visionary. He weaves intuition and wisdom into works that inspire us to reclaim our role as gay elders. *Our Tribe Chanting* combines powerful storytelling with practical exercises. Its guidance will allow you to embody his vision of what's possible for men who love men."

—**Oluwo Brian Olánipèkun Madigan**, creator of *The Orisa Vision Quests: Volume 1*

"What is a tribe? A gaggle of beings (possibly non-beings), a flock of similar intent, a pride of dissimilar intent which binds itself by its distinctions. There are as many tribes as there are stars in the firmament; there are as many beings within the tribes as we have taxonomies for their lapels. Does this not apply to every two-spirit auntie and uncle, wandering sadhu, salamander, owl, mountain, and ginkgo? And does not this lead us one step closer to life's ultimate query: Who am I? Professor Ramer gently directs us one lunge closer to the only possible solution: Who am I not?"

—**Gavin Geoffrey Dillard**, author of *The Comfort of Stone*

Our Tribe Chanting

Books by Andrew Ramer

From Wipf and Stock:

Two Flutes Playing

Two Hearts Dancing

Ever After

Texting with Angels

Fragments of the Brooklyn Talmud

Deathless

Torah Told Different

Queering the Text

Revelations for a New Millennium

The Spiritual Dimensions of Healing Addictions
& Further Dimensions of Healing Addictions
with Donna Cunningham

And:

Angel Answers

Ask Your Angels
with Alma Daniel and Timothy Wyllie

The Dream Gardener

for the men of our tribe
as we wander together
into an uncertain future

Contents

Foreword—by Toby Johnson | ix
An Acorn Chant | xiii

Wandering Through the Trees
The Paradoxical Power of Words | 3
My First GSV Keynote | 8

Splashing in a Stream
Paper Revery | 23
Into the Cauldron: Silence and Renewal | 28
Coming In: A Spiritual Guide to Daily Life in the Gay Tribe | 31
Food for the Soul: Queer Faith and Spirit | 38
Mentor and Mentors | 40
Animal, Vegetable, and Musical | 43
Sodom and Me: Queers and Fundamentalism | 48
The Consummate Friend | 54
Into Loving Arms | 58
Healthy Spirituality | 63
The Blessings of Our Elders—Is Pressed Into Our Cells | 66

CONTENTS

Swimming in the Lake
The Sacred Intimate Handbook | 75

Chanting in a Sacred Grove
Four Attunement Practices | 99
A Guided Meditation for Gay Sages | 103
The Awakening of Our Thymus Chakra | 107
A Time to Come Out and a Time to Come In | 112
Community Trust | 119
Eldering and Youngering | 124
Awakening the Elder Within | 127
Aligning with Your Sacred Earth Sages | 132
Thoughts for a Gathering | 135
Tayarti's Peace-Light Prayer | 137

Coda—Singing in the Arms of the Trees | 139
Author Bio | 145
Acknowledgments | 147

Foreword

Toby Johnson

YOU'RE ABOUT TO READ Andrew Ramer's *Our Tribe Chanting*—a wrap-around and weave-through of his two earlier books, *Two Flutes Playing* and *Two Hearts Dancing*. You'll be exploring a masterful example of the creation of a true myth for us queer gay folk. What my friend, who's now calling himself Eli, has written, is a myth for gay consciousness, a history in sacred time of how we men who love other men as equals, like us, came to be and came to accept our roles in fostering human evolution.

Like the great mythologist Joseph Campbell, the renowned comparative religions scholar and mythologist who I got to meet back in the 70s, Eli invites us as queer people to harness the power of myth as a way of coping with life and giving meaning and reason to our feelings of not fitting in and of having a secret about who we are. His work exemplifies Campbell's insight that the proper way to understand the age-old phenomena of mythology is from outside and above. The truth of a religious doctrine or myth isn't its historicity or factual accuracy but what it does to those who believe it, how it makes their lives better, how it gives meaning and emotional satisfaction to their experience, how it makes them compassionate, loving people. For us as queer people, "following our bliss,"—Campbell's most well-known aphorism—is a matter of survival and self-becoming: if we weren't following our bliss we wouldn't ever have become gay—or whatever you want to call it—in the first place.

I love Eli's idea that we have a special relationship with trees. Some people think of trees just as sources for wood to be cut down and made into houses and ships and firewood. But it was the evolution of trees in Earth's history that birthed the breathable atmosphere we all depend upon. Their giving themselves for our homes and for the fuel to cook our food is no small gift. And Eli reminds us over and over in this book of essays that, without being felled and hewn, trees provide us the natural cathedrals in which to converse with gods. How many of us have said we commune with God best out in nature? That we're better off taking a hike in the woods than going to a church to be exhorted by a professional preacher?

I love Eli's idea that we were here before God became a male and started pounding out rules. I love his idea that we can be storytellers and retell the history of humanity as it could have been—should have been—and not the way the historians of war and conquest have told us it was.

I love Eli's recounting that when asked in third grade who he wanted to be when he grew up he answered "Margaret Mead." Mead was the bisexual anthropologist who championed the idea that the sexual behaviors and beliefs of aboriginal peoples were fit study for ethnographic research. Eli reminds us that all queer people are parts of a network, an ocean, of consciousness, and reflect each other's insights and enlightenments.

In his autobiographical sketch *Memories of a Gay Catholic Boyhood*, gay historian John D'Emilio tells that in grad school he was literary and research assistant for Margaret Mead. Another of John's books is *Lost Prophet: the Life and Times of Bayard Rustin*. Rustin too was a ripple in our gay ocean and was nearly erased from history for that reason in spite of being a key organizer of the 1963 March on Washington. At one of those Gay Spirit Visions Conferences that Eli writes about, I was told by a wonderful old man named Harold Cole the secret that it was Rustin and gay white friends of Harold's who taught Rev. Martin Luther King,

Jr. about Mahatma Gandhi and non-violence. The Civil Rights Movement owes its most important political/spiritual/religious principle to gay men who had to hide their contribution to saving American society from racism and hatred. Gandhi, you know, was gay too. I say "you know" because the straight world doesn't know him that way, but we do.

I love that Eli tells us so much about GSV and Little Scaly Mountain. I bet some of you picked up this book because you too knew Eli from Gay Spirit Visions. And I love that he was wrapped as a babe in a yellow blanket. One of our great queer victories is over the polarization into male and female, masculine and feminine. We don't have to be one or the other. We can be both. We can be ourselves. We can make love as top or bottom. In fact, we can be both top and bottom at the same time.

Native Americans have given an identity to their sex- and gender-variant people as Two-Spirits, who have both a man's soul and a woman's soul and can move back and forth between them. Another of my own good fortunes was collaborating on a novel with anthropologist Walter L. Williams, who first introduced these ideas into modern gay thought with his 1986 book *The Spirit and the Flesh: Sexual Diversity in American Indian Culture*. Our novel is titled *Two Spirits*; it's a fictionalized tale about a real-life episode in Navajo/Diné history during the terrible years of the American Indian Wars.

Also writing about the Native American traditions was Will Roscoe. Like Eli, Will was a close friend of Harry Hay. His book about the historical person We'Wha, *The Zuni Man-Woman*, received the Margaret Mead Award in 1991 for helping to make anthropological data accessible to the wider public. (There she is again!) Will Roscoe has also helped create our own myths with books like *Queer Spirits: A Gay Men's Myth Book*. His broad-ranging *Jesus and the Shamanic Tradition of Same-Sex Love*, which I am pleased to have assisted Will in keeping in print, focuses on the love of equals as the essence of homosexuality.

I love that Eli asks us to meditate on being waves in an ocean of other gay waves and to sense that we are members of a time-transcending gay tribe. Fellow Jewish gay and JewBu spiritual writer Jay Michaelson introduced me to a wonderful story by yet another gay Jew Richard Alpert who came to be known as Ram Dass, a wiseman for all of American society with his book *Be Here Now*. The story goes something like this: Two waves are washing inexorably towards the shore; one says to the other, "I'm scared. All the other waves are crashing when they reach the beach." The other wave replies, "I can relieve your fears with just six words, but you have to listen very carefully and believe." The first wave resists at first, then finally asks what are the words. The second wave replies, "You're not a wave, you're water."

I love that Eli has shown us how to be that water—that gay water—and to make up stories like Ram Dass's to explain ourselves to ourselves and why we are different and queer and scare the bejeezus out of so many people—some of them our homosexual brothers and sisters.

Eli's work has been one of the great spiritual catalysts for soulful gay liberation in the last century; countless gay men have experienced a profound recognition of their own experience in his work, a sense of "me too" that resonates through their entire being. The book you hold in your hands completes his trilogy of queer mythology, gives us an illuminating perspective on the breadth and depth of his vision, and points us towards the next steps in the evolution of our community as queer people.

I love that I can call Eli Ramer my friend. And I hope, if only through these pages, that you, Dear Reader, can too.

> Toby Johnson is the author of *Gay Perspective: Things our [homo]sexuality tells us about the nature of God and the Universe, Gay Spirituality, Finding God in the Sexual Underworld, Finding Your Own True Myth: What I Learned from Joseph Campbell, Secret Matter*, and more. He is the former editor of White Crane Journal and the former production manager for Lethe Press and White Crane Books. You can learn more about his writings and teachings on gay/queer spirituality at his website—tobyjohnson.com.

An Acorn Chant

Soon after it came out my friend Don Shewey sent me his wonderful new book *Daddy Lover God,* a memoir of his journey as a sacred intimate. (You'll hear more about that later in this book.) Reading *Daddy Lover God* inspired me to go through decades of talks, essays, articles, sermons, poems, and channeled material to create this tree-companion to *Two Flutes Playing* and *Two Hearts Dancing,* neither of which you have to have read to read this one. Trees. And chanting. Because when I'm writing there's sound, vibration, chant inside, wind rustling leaves in the forest of my brain. Thank you Dr. Shewey—for our long friendship, your book, your engaging foreword to *Two Hearts Dancing,* and for inspiring me to create this book.

○

We may know something about our gay ancestors in Ancient Greece and other cultures around the world, but our history in modern times in the West isn't very long. In Munich in 1867 Karl Heinrich Ulrichs became the first person to speak out publicly in favor of homosexual rights. In 1897 German Jew Magnus Hirschfeld founded the first homosexual rights organization in the world, the Scientific Humanitarian Committee. In 1900 German writer Adolf Brand published the first issue of the first homosexual publication in the world. (We can talk about Germany later. Or not.)

When I was coming out in the early 1970s I met older men who hated the word gay. "We're homosexuals!" As a man in his seventies, I'm grounded in my own coming out history and continue to use the word "gay," although I have younger friends who don't like it. "I'm queer!" they say. So while I still use that word and will continue to do so in this book, I hope that it will be of interest to other men-who-love-men and to other queer folk too. And I invite you to journey through this book with others, if that's meaningful to you. To share it. To dance with it. Play with it. Chant through it, together.

○

I was born in 1951 in Elm/hurst, Queens, New York, across the street from an amusement park called Fairyland, and now live in Oak/land, California, up the street from an amusement park called Fairyland. That I'm a fairy, faerie, and that my first big crush in life was on the tall dark handsome pin oak in our Long Island backyard will tell you something about me as a lover of trees to this very day, and will give you some background into how the sections of this book were organized, and what's in them.

Imagine that you, that we, as a tribe of like-hearted men, are entering into a vast lush vibrant forest, wandering deeper and deeper into the intricately rooted and branch-uplifting trees. Yes. We wander, splash, swim, and then continue on till we get to the sacred grove that's the very heart of this blessed and blessing forest.

The first section of the book, **Wandering through the Trees**, is a thematic introduction that includes a poem and a talk I gave many years ago.

In **Splashing through a Stream**, the second section, you'll find information about who we are as a loving tribe, and find questions on how you can do your own sacred work in the world.

The third section, *Diving into the Lake*, contains the handbook about sacred intimates that's mentioned above, about sacred physicality, sacred sexuality.

Chanting in a Sacred Grove, the final section of the book, includes several rituals and practices you can do to deepen your own gay spiritual journey, and ends with an ancient prayer you're invited to give sound to, to chant, in whatever way you feel called to do. This short prayer also appears at the end of Two Flutes Playing.

Images, concepts, ideas, will appear here more than once, seen from different perspectives. Like the same kinds of trees in a forest. Each one unique. Leaves chanting in the wind. Trees. Chants. Stories. Sometimes the same one told in different ways. Like ravens and crows. Or not. Like pin oaks and pin stripes. Pin oaks and pine needles.

○

Take a slow soft breath. Notice your body and where you're sitting.

You can read the sections of this book in any order you feel called to.

Now look around you and take another soft slow tender breath.

When you are ready, you can go on reading. Later. Or now.

Now.

Yes, now.

In this time of deforestation and global challenges.

○

One third of the world's trees are threatened with extinction. There are now half as many animals in the wild as there were in 1970. Scientists tell us that someone born today will experience three times as many floods and droughts and seven times as many heat waves as someone who was born in 1950. And they estimate that by the year 2050 there will be one billion climate refugees around the world.

On this very different and frightening planet, how will we be able to stay connected, and how will we be able to heal our damaged home? By opening up to our sacred essential role as gay men, by deepening into the ancient wisdom of our queer ancestors, who lived in harmony with the planet for millennia, and by learning new behaviors and practices—which is what this chatty chanting little book is all about.

I first began to receive information from my guides in 1976, and continue to be an attentive and hopefully accurate scribe. Many of my guides were gay men when they were last embodied, and they taught me and have continued to repeat to me over the years (which you can read more about in *Two Flutes Playing* and *Two Hearts Dancing*) that for millennia the elders, shamans, seers, teachers, prophets, and healers for all of humanity were people who lived beyond the binary-gendered world of most of humanity. Yes. They lived like us, between female and male, night and day, matter and spirit, the living and the dead. And that's what my guides want us to ground ourselves in. Now. And to embody. That we are way-showers. Guides. For everyone. In this time when radical change is needed if we're going to survive and thrive on our home planet.

I and my guides and spirit companions thank you for joining us here. We celebrate your own innate gifts and hope that something in this odd little wandering chant-tree will help you to further embody your sacred gifts so that you can do your own healing work for the world and for all the living beings we share it with.

Wandering Through the Trees

The Paradoxical Power of Words

I invite you to step into the vibrating forest of words that is this book by reading it out loud, and as you do so, I and my guides invite you to think about your own seminal stories, your own world-wandering, your own embodied history. Because in this wobbly time, what can ground us and heal us and help to change the world—is the inspiring enlivening magic of words.

IN MY DREAM a teacher is reading to us from Tolstoy's *War and Peace*. Tolstoy, who liked men, if you pay careful attention to the sexy descriptions of the men he wrote about, to some of his early journal entries, and to what his wife had to say about him late in life. (I played with that in the story about him in my book *Ever After.*)

Only there was no dream. I made it up. But what is a story? A fabrication by any other name might be velvet, silk, or corduroy. On my father's side I come from a long line of tailors and seamstresses. Seems. My mother liked to say that I didn't have a first word. I had a first sentence. "No, I don't want to do that!"

In this poem a storyteller gets to play with light and darkness, with sounds and silence. Short silence after each dash and each period. Longer silence at the end of each sentence. Even longer at the end of each paragraph. And longer still....

I want to tell you that being read to is sometimes more delicious than sex.

OUR TRIBE CHANTING

○

In the dream a book of mine is published by a new press in a wonderful holographic edition. On the sacred essential role of gay men in the healing of the world. It gets reviewed in the *New York Times*. The reviewer hates it, but bad press sells books too, and it ends up on the *New York Times* best seller list. (My one big fantasy!)

After my father left home my mother bought a boxed set of all of Beethoven's symphonies. I hate when anyone calls them vinyl! They're records. Or phonograph records, if you want to be historically accurate. When no one was home I would blast them on our record player and dance wildly around the living room. Record player. Then phonograph, hi-fi, stereo. Yes, I played Beethoven, who loved young men. You can hear that in his music, if you are paying careful attention. Even more so in his later compositions, when he was deaf.

I don't like the word Queer, even though I used it in the title of one of my books, *Queering the Text*. When I was teaching a class in my synagogue I wrote on the whiteboard in the lobby: "Kweer Torah Study—second floor." I don't like the Q word. Not because it was one of the worst things to call someone when I was growing up. I don't like it because it means "strange, different," and when we use it we unconsciously invoke the majority, the mainstream, the ones who aren't us, while "gay" for me and my generation means "happy, joyful" and invites a connection to the ones who are like us, who might want to love us.

The sound of water splashing over rocks is one of my favorite sounds in the world.

○

In the dream a young student in a writing class that I'm teaching on Zoom makes up a word to replace Queer. A word that names us, invokes just only us, and references no one else. It catches on like "they" and "them" and I am very happy.

THE PARADOXICAL POWER OF WORDS

In 2012 I was ordained a maggid, a storyteller in the Jewish tradition. When I told my family about it they all said, "Of course." In my dream the book I wrote gets translated into a universal language like Esperanto but lovelier. (Universal? Really? Isn't that a bit of an exaggeration? Wouldn't "global" be a better word?) The day we moved for the first time, I left my globe of the world on the living room floor by accident, just inside the door of our little apartment in Elmhurst, Queens. I was five. Mommy said I could take it with me in the car. Richie took his teddy. But Daddy refused to go back for my globe, even when I started crying in back seat. He said he had to follow the moving van. (The sound of a car or truck engine is one of my least favorite sounds in the world. Along with the banging of a metal screen door.)

Queens. Almost like queers. But not quite.

Among my favorite smells—you. And forsythia, lilac, lily-of-the-valley, hyacinth, salvia, lavender, rosemary. I rub my fingers on their leaves and raise them to my nose and inhale deeply, when I'm out for a walk and pass one on my path.

A story is a song that's sitting down, not standing up.

○

In the dream the old man is writing a poem. On the wall above his desk hangs a copy of Jules Bastien-Lepage's painting of Joan of Arc, staring out into space, clearly listening to the three golden saints who are floating in the air behind her. Jules Bastien-Lepage, who loved other men. You can feel it in his tender brushstrokes. His painting changed my life the first time I saw it. Big as the wall it was hanging on, in the Metropolitan Museum of Art in New York City. I was seven or eight. Hearing voices in my head but not telling anyone. But looking at that painting I could see Joan listening to the three glowing figures floating in the trees behind her. And I knew for the first time in my life I wasn't the only one to do that.

Bliss. I asked my daddy who she was. "Joan of Arc." Never heard of her. Knew enough to not ask who she was. Daddy would have said, "What do you mean you don't know who she was?

Everyone knows about Joan of Arc!" Three days of bliss. Then I said, "Daddy, remind me who that lady was in the painting." He told me. Her whole life story. How she wore men's clothing. How she died. And terror rose up in me. And it took twenty years till I was ready to open up again to my voices. Perhaps you've read their words in other of my books. And lots of other books of other people's listening too.

Listening.

Hearing.

Here-ing.

"Sticks and stones can break my bones but names will never harm me" we used to say when I was a kid.

I miss the word "fag." No one seems to use it anymore. In the poem in my dream that wasn't a dream there are two fags. Once is dancing. And one is not. He is watching the other man. Smiling. And I think that man is you. Yes. I'm certain of it.

o

My father didn't stop the car and go back to get my globe, but he gave me a gift a few years later, understanding me better than I was yet able to do. I was around fifteen and we were back in the Metropolitan Museum of Art, some years after my encounter with Joan of Arc, to see a show of ancient cave art. I was deeply moved by it and as we were walking out he said to me, "Who do you think painted those paintings?" I had no idea and said so. "Well, the men were out hunting and fishing. The women were cooking and taking care of the children. They must have been painted by the fags, who looked around at the cave they were living in and said: "This cave is ugly. I think we should decorate it!'"

His answer changed how I lived in the world. A kind of globe re-gifting. Thank you, Jack.

In the dream. It's the middle of the night. The lights are out. The young man licking his lover's left armpit, the one who wrote this story, cannot speak now. But you can hear him breathing. As he stretches out on pale blue satin sheets. Blue of sky. When the sun is stretching and preparing to rise.

Silence . . .

Sigh lens . . .

. . . .

_—.—.—.—.—.—-

_____!

My First GSV Keynote

Was it 1988? A letter arrived in the mail from someone I didn't know: Raven Wolfdancer. He'd read a photocopy of my unpublished book *Two Flutes Playing*. That letter led to others, then phone calls that went on for hours, which grew into a deep friendship. Raven was a gifted gardener, artist, healer, visionary, and one of the founders of GSV, the Gay Spirit Visions Conference, along with Ron Lambe and Peter Kendrick, and he invited me to speak at the first gathering, along with Harry Hay and Franklin Abbott. I was nervous to go, a shy fellow not yet forty, intimidated by the thought of speaking with Harry, co-founder of the Mattachine Society in 1950, the first sustained homosexual rights group in the United States, and of the Radical Faeries in 1970. But I said yes and traveled from Brooklyn, New York to Highlands, North Carolina to attend the First Annual Celebrating Gay Spirit Visions Conference which was held from November 2nd to 4th in 1990 at the Mountain Retreat Center. That gathering changed my life. I ended up going to GSV for the next twenty years, spoke or presented at every conference, and became the only person who had a perfect attendance record for those first twenty years.

There were around 75 of us at that gathering in the lush green mountains. Harry spoke first, then I spoke, then Franklin did. We shared meals, danced together, and had a very moving Heart Circle in which we shared with each other our deepest thoughts and feelings. Some of the men I met there have remained friends to this very day, including Don Shewey. At the end of the conference Harry came up to me, put his hands on my shoulders and said, "I want to bless you as a younger elder of the tribe." Then he leaned forward and stuck his tongue in my mouth. Furious, I was about to push him away—when I saw pouring into his back a cone of bright yellow energy about twenty feet long, that filled his entire body and poured out of his tongue into my mouth, filling me from head to toe with that same bright yellow light. Wow! is all that I can say. (Yellow. Both chicken-color. Scared. And the color of the blanket the nurses wrapped me in when I was born, which you can read about in *Two Hearts Dancing,* with illustrations by Raven Wolfdancer.) And here I am, all these years later, no longer a younger elder, in my seventies as Harry was then, still doing my work and still feeling amusedly blessed by his blessing.

Harry and I continued to be in touch from that time on, and toward the end of his life he and his partner John Burnside lived a block away from me in San Francisco. I wasn't part of the amazing team of loving gay men who supported them as Harry moved toward death, but I would visit them from time to time and Harry and I always had long intense and engaging conversations about gayness and our sacred roles in the world. Another blessing!

Harry, Franklin, and my talks were published in a small booklet called *Visions of Gay Spirit,* created by Raven, illustrated by Randy Taylor, produced by Gary Kaupman at Southern Voice, and published by Stepping Stone Press in Atlanta, Georgia, in 1991. I've transcribed my talk below (which I sometimes think of as my best talk) as a way of stepping into the forest of this book. (Or is it a jungle?) Occasionally you'll find added comments on the talk in italics, in parentheses.

The Talk

I have a lot of things I want to say, but I thought it would be nice to start out with all of us getting tuned together. So let's close our eyes and put our hands on our hearts. Just feel your heart beating and know that all of us are beating together. That the river of life that runs through us is the same, beating and beating and beating. And feel the life of your heart in your hands, beating, pulsing. Let us reach out and join hands for a moment, and feel in the hands of your brothers the same river of life, beating. Feel your breath in your body rising and falling. Just let your hands rise and fall with this beat, this ocean that carries us all together. Let us be all together, floating on this ocean of life, on the same raft, on the same journey, the same current, rising and falling, and rising again together. Take a moment to look in the eyes of the men whose hands you have been holding, greet them. Look around the room and know that for this time here we are all traveling on the same raft together.

How I got to do the work that I do, I realized several day ago, began when I was in third grade. We had to give a talk in class about who in all of history we wanted to be if we could be anyone else. People picked George Washington and Caesar and a lot of people picked baseball players and film stars. I picked Margaret Mead. *(Who lived from 1901 to 1978.)* This caused a great deal of trouble. My parents were called to the school because in third grade you are not supposed to know about Margaret Mead. And it was highly inappropriate as a gender choice although it was better than if I had said Marilyn Monroe. I think I understood even in third grade that we were on similar journeys, long before anyone knew about Mead's bisexuality, about what personally impelled her to wander the planet investigating other cultures.

That was in a sense the beginning of a journey as a man who loves men. I was asking a question all by myself, completely in isolation, which was "What am I? Who am I? Where do I come from? Where am I going?" That's the question that all of us ask, in community and in isolation. "How did I get to be here in this way that is different from the people around me?" I don't think that I had any sense in third grade that my journey as an anthropologist, which was part of my training, was going to take me in a kind of shamanic direction, into what could be called psychic anthropology, yet that is where it went.

When I was a college radical we took over the computer building. *(At U. C. Santa Barbara, in 1971.)* The computer was not quite as wide as this room, and much longer. It was enormous. And now you can do exactly the same work in much less time on a little laptop that you can throw in your backpack. So there is something about who we are as a people which is shamanic, that used to take a very long time. We had to drum for hours, and maybe put consciousness altering substances in our bodies. But I think the same way that you can get a little tape recorder, *(I've had younger students who had no idea what a tape recorder is!)* where they used to be huge, and a computer that is little, that an accumulation of all the work we've done over time has allowed us to travel very quickly without any rituals.

As an anthropologist, *(Figuratively. Metaphorically. I went to college to become an archaeologist and ended up with a degree in Religious Studies from Berkeley)* I found myself going back to the end of the Ice Ages. Again, and again, and again, in dreams, with all of my guides, and in channeling. Actually I don't like the word channeling. I have friends and teachers who don't have physical bodies, and I talk to them and I dialogue with them and I write down what they are saying. That to me isn't channeling, that to me is a relationship, the same way that we *(here I looked at Raven)* talked on the phone and wrote letters. I didn't know who you were, and yet I know you. My journey has been with people who don't have physical bodies, and they keep talking to me about the end of the Ice Ages. For two reasons. One, is that we are at the end of a major cycle in history. We have reached the point where we are capable of destroying the planet. This cycle of history began at the end of the time when the planet was working on destroying us, if you look at the Ice Ages that way. And when that time ended and the ice began to recede, we started a cycle of history that ends now. You can't have an end without going back to the beginning and tying it all up together.

So this concerns all of us as human beings, but it also concerns us as members of the Gay tribe, because our history began 10,000 years ago at the end of the Ice Ages. For the first time there was space for people to spread out, and very new questions were being asked. It was no longer absolute, pure survival. We had the opportunity to explore the planet, to explore consciousness, and it was in that time that we as a tribe began to define ourselves.

The vision that I want to share with you is about what I call the "main body of the tribe," or the tribe of all tribes. It moves very slowly across the planet through consciousness. Its job is bringing new life, creating homes, nurturing the young. As any body that moves very slowly discovers, it can send out tentacles to look ahead, to look over the next hill, to see where it is going, what is happening next. So at the end of the Ice Ages different tribal groups began to emerge, and we were one of them. I call these groups consciousness scouts. We have many allies who are other kinds of consciousness scouts. We as Gay people wander off into consciousness in one direction. We are closely allied to the tribe of women who love women, who wander out of the main body of the tribe in another direction. Our job isn't the same. Recently a friend of mine called and said to me, "I was reading where there is a newsletter for Lesbians who raise goats." He said, "I have known Gay men who have raised goats." But he said that the thought that there are so many Lesbians raising goats that they needed a newsletter is something that is not us. We don't do this, we don't raise goats in such great numbers.

For a long time we have thought as an oppressed minority that our real natural allies were other minority people. I think our real allies include the Deaf nation, and the Blind nation, which in their own different ways are discovering that they have a language—and that they are a people—in the same way that we do and are. There is something about me that I have in common with all of you, even through we've just met. We don't have a good word for handicapped, crippled, disabled people—another consciousness tribe. All of us are going out into consciousness, exploring very different directions. But we are doing it, not for ourselves alone, but what we do—and I think we sometimes forget this—is to bring back the information we discover to the main body of the tribe.

What has happened in our lifetime, and for the last several thousand years, is that the main body of the tribe has disenfranchised all consciousness scouts. It has institutionalized us, locked us away. It has said that we are marginal, we are cripples, we are partial people. Instead of saying, "Gee, there was once a time when the healers of the planet were Blind," or "Gay people have a certain power."

The coming together of what it was that made us a people happened at the end of the Ice Ages. We began to isolate what is our nature, how it is separate, where we are scouting. One of the things that we were called at the end of the Ice Ages was the "Stand Between People." We stand between genders. We stand between the living and the dead. We stand between matter and spirit. Our job is to scout that terrain for the main body of the tribe, and to bring back all that information for the main body of the tribe. *(Sometimes my guides called them, called us, "the Walks-Between People" too, as they did in this book's companion volumes.)*

I think what we have been doing in the last 20, 30, 40, 50 years is coming together as a community, at times forgetting that we build bridges from the furthest edges of consciousness back to the main body of the tribe. It is out of the main body of the tribe that all of us emerged. And the next generation of Gay men will emerge from the main body of the tribe to join us.

What we step into before we are born, every one of us, is not just a physical experience, but also in the collective consciousness, which at this point is mostly collectively unconscious. It is a real energetic field that has two aspects to it. One is that it is very much like a telephone network. There are telephone lines that wrap around the planet. *(How curiously dated this sounds, in an age of cell phones, the internet, and wireless technology. But it's still true in part for me. I don't use a cell phone!)* And then there are the repair people, the maintenance people, the operators, the technicians. There is always an interface between the technology and the human beings. It exists in the same way in the collective unconscious, that there is information, pure lines of information, that are held together by non-physical people. At the end of the Ice Age there were people from our tribe who chose not to incarnate again but to remain "out there," holding together these pieces of information, holding together the consciousness of the tribe. And they remain there still. And as we end this cycle of history, I think more and more of us are beginning to recognize that there is some kind of guidance, there is someone out there who has been working with us, that we are not alone. Also, as the cycle ends, those beings get to retire, and we may become the next generation of ancestors who hold together this consciousness when we leave our bodies.

I want to remind you of something that all of you all know about inside, which is how it was 10,000 years ago, when our mothers were pregnant with us. Before we were born they could hear how we were tuned. They knew that we were going to emerge from their bodies as men who love men. Our tuning was not the same as the tuning of men who love women. Vibrationally we are not the same. Anatomically we might be the same, but I don't think we are in every sense. And as Harry was saying last night, there may be things within the brain itself that are not the same. But 10,000 years ago our mothers knew that we were different, and they knew that part of their bringing us into the world was also about giving us up. We are talking about a time when there may have been only 3 million people on the planet. But living out in the woods were little communities of men who loved men. And they knew we were showing up, they could hear that another one is about to be born. "Forty miles down the coast, I can hear him coming." And at some point, after we were weaned, three four, five, six years later, two men who were lovers wandered out of the hills wrapped in whatever kind of clothing people wore—sewn together, dyed elk skin?—wandered down and came to the house, the hut, the cave, the village, the thatched dwelling that our biological parents lived in. They had been waiting for these people who came out of the woods. They knew that this child was on loan only, that it belonged to those men who lived in the woods.

||||

Growing up, it was a great thing to have a doctor in the family. "This is my son, the doctor." Well, in those days, if you had a Gay son it gave you a lot of clout, a lot of power. Everyone was really excited. When a woman knew that she was carrying one of our people, that was a blessing to her family, to her clan, to her tribe, because it gave them a reel-in to a whole other level of power, of wisdom, of consciousness. So there was a great celebration when we were given over to the men who came out of the woods from the mountains to take us back home, to what we knew was home. Some part of us knew, "This is what I was born into, but this is not my destiny. This is not my journey. This is the only way on this planet to get here. But now I am going out there to live with these men and become as they are, a consciousness scout for the main body of the tribe." So, we carry this information whether or not we have been Gay in any other life, or whether or not we believe that we have ever had any other life. This information sits, lives, pulsates in the collective unconscious.

I grew up in Orange County, California, *(No quite. We moved there from Long Island, New York when I was sixteen. But what comes next is accurate. I was quite often the target of verbal anti-Semitism by other boys in school and even from a teacher who wouldn't let me talk in his class.)* where it wasn't even safe to be Jewish so there was no way I was going to come out. But I knew all kinds of things about who I was, and I think we all did because it is out there in the collective unconscious. So we have several jobs, and Harry spoke about them last night. *(Including cutting through layers of guilt and shame, exploring our sacred sexuality and connecting with Spirit.)* One of the jobs that human beings have as an incarnate species is that most other life forms are horizontal. Birds are sort of oblique, but most other life forms are aligned with the planet itself. We are vertical, not all the time, but a good deal of the time. So what we are doing is not just drawing energy up from the planet, but drawing energy down from the heavens and up from the planet, and weaving it together. All human beings are weavers. But the frequency that men who love men weave together is even more purely vertical, phallic, aligned. That is a frequency which we share with one other major life form on this planet, which is the Standing People, the trees.

One of our most ancient jobs was that we were considered the guardians of the trees at the end of the Ice Ages. We were the ones who could go into a community and say, "You can cut these trees, you can't cut those, you can use this wood, you can't use that." We didn't do this from an intellectual sense, we did it because we dialogued with the trees. We dialogued with the tree spirits and this I think is perfectly clear in our history now, whether we are conscious of it or not. You can go to any city on the planet Earth and where will you find other gay men? In a park. It is not just because it is dark and secluded. Some of it has to do with the tree themselves and our relationship to the trees. This goes back to Lesbians and goats. Women who loved women were the guardians of the animals not the trees. They had a different job. So this was a big part of our job, that we talked to the trees. We made remedies from flowers, from plants, we were the ones that began to carve things, and much of the art that we still work with comes from this ancient capacity to use the trees. Paint was made out of tree products, plant products. So who painted the cave paintings during the Ice Ages? Who went to Lascaux? I think it was the men who were not out killing each other, out hunting. It was the men who stayed home. Although I think there were also Gay warriors and always will be. But our job now is to become more involved as a community in working with our brothers the trees—planting trees, working politically, ecologically, whatever ways we find resonate with our energy, because we are still the guardians of the trees and no one else is. The Sierra Club does great work, but it is our job and we have to own it again.

Another way that we were a Stand-Between People was that we stood between the living and the dying. And the way that women and women's communities were the midwives for birthing, all men, but especially Gay men, were midwives for the dying. When it was time to die, the people in the main body of the tribe called us. We were the ones who held their hand, we were the ones who spoke to their spirit companions on the other side and said, "This person is coming," and said to the person who was dying, "On the other side will be three beings. This is what they look like. This is where you are going, this is how it will feel." So it's no accident that we as a community have invited into our midst a dying that is teaching all of us how to be midwives again. As painful, as difficult as it is to live through this time, we invited it back to remind us of our power. This is a very big part of our work. I think we are all doing it in different ways. Each of us has a different piece of that journey, whether it is to write about it, whether it is to change someone's bedpan, hold someone's hand, research new cures. I think the more that we remember that we are midwives for the dying, the more that we bring in an energy that will transmute whatever it is that AIDS is.

It's part of the nature of maleness. Women stand at the opening door, men stand at the end. And I think that part of the journey that men have gone on after the end of the Ice Ages has been to ask the question, "What does it mean to die, what does it mean to kill, how can I best explore that?" Once you know that on a certain level the soul is immortal, it doesn't make it right to go out and kill people, but it makes it a part of the science of asking, "What does it mean to have a body and then not to have one? What does it mean that I had a body ten seconds ago and then your spear went right through my chest and now I don't have that body? What does it mean that my sword just chopped off your head?" We have been asking that question for so long that we all know the answers.

What Harry said last night about our job, our work, our vision, and about what we bring to the community—is our capacity to love. What we bring to the community of men, as men, because we remain men, is a level of tenderness that men in the main body of the tribe have learned to be afraid of. It is like a fire brigade, a bucket brigade. Way out there at the farthest end of consciousness, there are men who love men who are almost drowning in intimacy, not afraid of it. They fill up these buckets and they pass them back and the bucket keeps working down the line. And out there someplace is the main body of the tribe of men, who are afraid of us because they are defined by limitations that we're not, in our loving tribe of man-clans. There are the men way out, way way out there, who have nothing to do with gender at all. They are neither male nor female. They are something other. Utterly other. Then there are clans of us that are male and female and define ourselves in those ways. And then there are men among us who also love women and then there are men among us in our tribe who say clearly, "I am exactly like the men in the main body of the tribe except for what I do in bed." They are the people who are closest to the main body of the tribe. They are the ones in our tribe who get the buckets last. They are the ones sitting in an office. Everything about them is straight except that one sleeps with a woman and one sleeps with a man. The guy who sleeps with men is the last person to get the bucket. He is the one who has to pass it on to his heterosexual workmate in whatever way he knows how, in whatever way he can best come up with to say to this man—"Listen, on a planet that could at any moment destroy itself, we have outgrown the scientific experiment to understand what it means to kill each other. We know exactly what it means to kill each other. We also are learning what it means to kill an entire planet, we know this." So our job really is to be what some of my non-physical friends have called "trans-political espionage agents." Some of us have to be flamboyant and very much out there, but others of us really have to be trans-political espionage agents and pass for straight so that the other guys in the locker room can get some of our energy, our tenderness, our capacity to be open to the heart and not be afraid of it.

We started doing this job almost 10,000 years ago. There are places on the planet where we never stopped doing it. But for much of western history we were denied our power, were denied our vision, we were told that we did not exist as a people. Yet we all know that we are a people, we are not a people necessarily born to like-parents. The same way the Blind nation is not necessarily born to Blind parents. The same way the Deaf nation is not necessarily born to Deaf parents, and yet we are a people as they are a people. And all of us at the same time are discovering our peopleness, which I think is very wonderful because, here we are.

The moment I arrived here there was a recognition—"These are my people." Some of it is visual. We spend a lot of time as men looking at each other and having visual clues. Wasn't it Oscar Wilde, green ties, or something like that? *(Note from Toby Johnson. "It was green carnations.")* Visual clues are important at certain times, but how we really recognize each other is by how we sound. We don't vibrate the same way as non-Gay men. The more clearly we step into our power as men who love men (and not everyone has to do this, there are men who stand equally between loving men and loving women, and there are men who go back and forth) but when we as a tribe step clearly into our own power, our body vibrates differently. You can be in a room of 50,000 people and you will hear, not see, you will hear the other Gay men in that room. And so some of our job is to keep our eyes closed more often because we tend to judge each other a lot by how we look. But the eye of the heart is in darkness, it doesn't see the light, it sees in the darkness, it hears. How we meet each other as intimates, as partners, as lovers, as companions, is from what we hear in the silence, in the darkness.

So we are guardians of the trees and midwives for the dying. We are artists and visionaries and healers and shamans and journeyers about to step in to create a new cycle of history. Part of our job now, part of why we are here, is to create a legacy for our heirs. We who are living out in the woods are preparing ourselves to welcome new generations of men who love men. All of us were born into pain, denial, fear, and now generations of men are being born into death and fear. Our job is to create a powerful, loving community of men. None of us were welcomed into our tribe. This is our major job now, to clarify who we are so that we can welcome the succeeding generations, so that we become the grandfathers that we're just beginning to discover exist in our midst. There are so few grandfathers and so many of us. Our job now is to make certain that the men who follow us will have all of us as grandfathers.

There is a part of us that loves youth, but I would like to spend the next several days as very old men who remember what we remember as very old men. I mean as very old men in these bodies, but also very old men who remember that we have a history that began 10,000 years ago. So as you are wandering in the trees, as you are eating, as you are encountering each other, let some part of you know that you are very, very, very old. We *are* very old, we *are* very wise and we know very clearly who we are, and always have because we were born into this pattern in the collective unconscious. What we are doing is making something conscious that we knew all along. We knew we were a people, we knew we were different, we knew that we had a function, we know that we were going somewhere. And here we are!

Splashing in a Stream

Paper Revery

The Bible begins with an origin story. Perhaps we all have one. Can you remember the first boy you were attracted to? The first youth? The first man? Can you remember when you first sensed that you were "different"? Was it an internal sense or something that was said to you by someone else? "What kind of boy are you?" "You're not a boy you're a girl?" Or . . .

These stories shape and sometimes make us, and as I read through my old work, inspired by Don's amazing stories, I kept coming back to this one, which doesn't begin with my first big boy-crush—a classmate down the street when I was in around fifth grade whose lithe body and stride made me want to touch him. Or the cousin a generation older—whose warm smile and deep voice did the same thing to me. Or the occasional pictures of never-fully-naked men that I found in magazines that got me hard, that I would clip out and hide in a wooden knife box in the back of my bedroom closet, to be taken out at night and flipped through as I played with my hard penis that eventually began to spout a thick liquid, which gave me even more pleasure. No, this story, while grounded in those earlier stories, begins later—and in sharing it with you

I hope it will evoke your own foundational stories of self, and how you grew from them.

RFD—Issue 175, Fall 2018

NEWLY OUT OF HIGH school, June 1969, Anaheim, California. Spending the summer with my father and his wife in New York. The morning after the Stonewall Uprising a neighbor called to tell my stepmother—"The fags rioted last night on Christopher Street." After breakfast we walked over. There was rubble in the streets, scared cops on horseback, and we passed my favorite candy store, one wall lined with racks of magazines, hundreds of them. Afternoons I would wander over to casually flip through one after another till I'd worked my way to *After Dark*, which covered the theatre, film, dance, and art scene. Unlike the athletes in *Sports Illustrated*, there were pages of men, often shirtless, never touching each other, and—sexy! Standing there with men all around me, only men, I would memorize images for that night's in-the-shower masturbation adventure—too afraid to ever look at any of the men around me, usually older, and too afraid to ever buy a single issue.

A senior in Berkeley. 1973. I remember wandering into Moe's Books on Telegraph Avenue and seeing in the New Releases section, face out, a book with a circular rainbow on the cover—*The Gay Liberation Book* by Len Richmond and Gary Noguera, unlike anything that I'd ever seen. For about a week I went in every day to look at it, letting my fingers quickly stroke the cover, too afraid to take it off the shelf. Then one day it was gone and I wandered through every section of the store till I found it upstairs, in a corner, in the Sociology section, I think. Standing in that corner with my back to the aisle, I read the entire book, too afraid to buy it, not to mention too poor—that book an essential part of my coming out process.

I was twenty-four before I ever saw a picture of two men kissing—on a flyer for a gay dance that was stapled to a lamppost. By then I was living in New York again, in another part of Manhattan, with my father and a different stepmother. A year out of college and having broken up with my first boyfriend, you might have expected that I'd eventually move into my first apartment in the Village. But I was a boy who (my parents delighted in embarrassing by telling his few friends) was sent home from the hospital wrapped in a yellow blanket, not a blue one or even a pink one. So yes, I had boyfriends, loved to visit the Oscar Wilde Bookshop on Christopher Street, where I looked through and sometimes even bought gay magazines, newspapers, and books—where I spent as much time on the lesbian side as on the gay side.

In those days, because I didn't smoke, drink, or do drugs, loved to dance but hated loud music, I never went to gay bars or clubs, and only went to the baths twice. I continued to read gay publications like *Fag Rag* and *Christopher Street*, and it was *Gay Community New,* from Boston that shaped my political opinions—but I also read *Amazon Quarterly* from cover to cover, along with *Lilith, Off Our Backs,* and other feminist and lesbian magazines, and found myself having far more in common culturally with the lesbians I met than with the gay men I met and dated. So when it was time to go out on my own, instead of finding a place in the gay Village, I moved across the river to lesbian Park Slope in Brooklyn, where I lived for nineteen years in the same two room apartment one building in from Prospect Park.

For six of those years I worked in the Community Bookstore, two blocks away and around the corner from my apartment, and while I met several of my boyfriends in that time, my social circle was almost entirely composed of lesbians, several of whom I still count among my dearest friends. Among that circle of friends and acquaintances were the founders of the feminist press Out & Out Books, Joan Larkin, Elly Bulkin, Jan Klausen, and Irena Klepfisz, all of whose books I devoured. I remember evenings, often the only man, sitting in Joan's living room with Audre Lorde, June Jordan, and Adrienne Rich, listening to them talk about writing, politics, and also about their spiritual lives—something that none of the gay men I knew would talk about till the coming of AIDS. And one night in her kitchen, Joan tapped me on my shoulders with a thick wooden spoon whose handle was almost a yard long—and dubbed me an honorary lesbian, which to this day I rank as one of the great honors of my life.

I devoured the journals, poetry, and fiction of lesbian author May Sarton, who became a pen pal, along with the works of Virginia Woolf, Simone de Beauvoir, Monique Wittig, and other women writers, including Alice Walker, who lived for a time in the neighborhood and sometimes came into the store. I helped my boss, a straight woman, set up the store's Women's Section and helped her maintain a flourishing shelf of local and regional woman authors, many of them self-published, all of them essential to me.

Not into drag or drag shows, I dressed and moved in the world like my lesbian friends. My identity makes more sense to me today than it did back then, when the world was more binary. And now, in a time when porn is everywhere, when you can find sex on your phone in an instant, when there are fewer and fewer gay bookstores left, in fact fewer and fewer bookstores at all, I remember with joy and gratitude the 1970s, when gay and lesbian presses were thriving, when there were magazines and newspapers that talked about us and our lives in ways that we had never seen before. And when I think about my own work as a writer, it is that time and those women's books and periodicals that made me possible—a gay (not queer, although I sometimes use the word) man in his late sixties who's a Goddess worshipper and an honorary lesbian, who spent the last eight months slowly reading out loud before he got in bed each night the collected poems of Emily Dickinson, all 1789 of them. His favorite is 1775, which he's also set to music:

> To make a prairie it takes a clover and one bee,
> One clover, and a bee,
> And revery.
> The revery alone will do,
> If bees are few.

He is now reading out loud a new verse translation of the *Bhagavad-Gita*.

- If you feel called to do so, take out a pad and pen or pencil, and make a quick list of your own gay history, queer history.
- Have you ever done this before?
- If you do it, and you have or haven't done this before, what does it look and feel like to read through your list?
- Did anyone share their stories with you as you were moving toward coming out, as you were coming out?
- If they did, what did it mean to you in your unfolding journey?
- If no one shared their story or stories with you, imagine how your journey might have been different if someone had?
- What books, poems, songs, films, classes, discussions, websites and apps were a part of your journey?
- How did they help to shape, direct, inspire, and change you?
- Look over your notes again and think about the people you can share it with, and send it out to them.
- Know that your story is essential and that everyone who hears it will be inspired by it to perhaps write their own list and share it, for our history as a tribe is needed by all of humanity.

Into the Cauldron: Silence and Renewal

October 2018 at the Stone and Stang Gay Men's Gathering

These words feel like ancient history to me now, as I sit typing in 2024. Although Covid is fading around us, at seventy-three and with lung damage I'm more at risk than others for being exposed to the flu and all kinds of other things, and the idea of being at a real, live, fully in-person gathering—smiling and hugging and eating and dancing with other men—seems like a dream, like ancient history. Was I really once sitting in a room in the glorious Santa Cruz Mountains? Apparently I was. And what happened there, as I read through it again, feels as important a message as it did when I wrote the words you're about to read, and when I delivered them to a warm wonderful loving group of men gathered together to learn and grow, to connect and celebrate who we are. Written and delivered by me, they are for and about—You!

I'M DEEPLY HONORED AND delighted to be here, as someone who thinks of himself as a gregarious recluse.

In the past we often placed wisdom and power outside of ourselves, in leaders and rulers rather than within ourselves, but the journey that I want to share with you is one of embodied elderhood for all human beings, in our time and in the future.

Where are we?—on Father Earth—the significance and importance of that, lodged in 100,000 and more years of human experience and lodged in the depths of our psyches. Where is Father Earth?—birthed like all worlds from Mother Sky. She, what we now think of as God, is never separate from Her creation, birthed from her Self.

Physicality is holy. The universe is holy, Planet Earth is holy, all of us are holy. We are all immortal souls who have chosen to become physical for a time because being in a body is a perfect training ground in which immortal souls can connect and grow.

This is a pivotal time in human history. If we're going to survive and thrive, and if sustainable life upon this planet is going to continue, all of us must remember that we've chosen to be here, now, and we must remember our own piece of the puzzle. Human evolution is happening, in our physical bodies. We are living on the cusp of the interface between cellular reality and our souls. In the past it was our minds that led us, but in this time, as my spiritual director Janice Farrell likes to say—"The body leads the way."

Some of us began our cycles of incarnation here and others on other world. Most of us who are queer today started off somewhere else. My guides tell me that there are around 160,000,000 resident aliens engaged in sharing the information we brought, and that there are approximately 120,000 others like me, Earth Oracles, doing information sharing.

What I was told in June 2017 is that there is a 93.8 % chance/probability of humanity creating a positive future. As of today that number has not gone down, in spite of how things look in this nation and around the world.

So, whether or not you think or know of yourself as a resident alien, all of us are transformational agents.

○

- Take out your pad and pen or pencil again. Now inhale slowly, exhale even more slowly, and write down these words and then say them:

- "I am a transformational agent"
- Take a few moments to answer the questions below.
- How did you feel saying these words?
- Did you say them out loud, quietly to yourself, or silently within?
- Did you believe them to be true?
- What is your work as a transformational artist?
- If doubts came up for you, what were they and where did they come from?
- Did you feel any excitement in saying them?
- Any fear?
- What can you do in your life, in your practices, in your communities, to deepen and expand your needed work?

Coming In: A Spiritual Guide to Daily Life in the Gay Tribe

The chorus of a 1976 song by a group called the Bee Gees that begins with "How a love so right can turn out to be so wrong," my brain instantly turns into, "How a love so wrong can turn out to be so right." (Only much later did someone tell me that the song was written for the group's closeted gay manager.) And so, in a different way, if someone asks me "How did you come out?" some part of my brain will always turn that into, "How did you come in?"

You just rang the doorbell and I've just come to the door, opened it, and I'm smiling at you, so very glad that you're here. "Welcome, my dear. Please Come In!"

It's been half a century since the Stonewall Uprising, not the first one of its kind but the one that in most accounts marks the birth of the American gay liberation movement. In this time we've seen the emergence of gay communities and gay organizations, the election of openly gay leaders, lived with the devastation of AIDS and dealt with our continuing struggles to achieve equal rights for ourselves and other queer people. Sadly, today in places around the world, to my surprise and dismay, the situation for gay and queer people isn't getting better, safer—but worse—as religious leaders and politicians are speaking out and acting out against us

Our movement has been viewed through a social and political lens since its inception, but I'm inviting you to look at the ways in which being gay is a spiritual phenomenon. In the West we think of God as something definable, but in some traditions what we call God is spoken of as The Great Mystery. Ultimately our spiritual lives bear witness to this Mystery. Doctors and scientists, psychologists and theologians, continue to debate about genetics, hormones, social and environmental factors, without coming to any clear conclusions about who we are and how we became what we are. We may never have answers to these questions, and they may not really matter, for we gay men are here and have been for as long as there have been human beings. Perhaps we need to accept the fact that our origins are mysterious because we're rooted in Mystery, and consciously connecting with Mystery—is a spiritual journey.

A Time To Come Out and a Time To Come In

Many of us Come Out when we recognize ourselves as sexual beings, and acknowledge the truth about our sexual preference. Coming Out to ourselves and others can also coincide with our joining a gay group or club or when we walk into a gay bar for the first time. Coming Out is a rite of passage that straight folk don't have to go through. It's one of the few authentic ones in our time, even if we do it in a very private way.

As we move deeper into a new century and millennium, it's time for us to also have Coming In rituals, where we step into the community of Gay men, into the culture of Gay men. As our peoplehood is increasingly being recognized, it's time for us to celebrate who we are in ways that don't define us solely by our sexuality, although that's a joyously vital part of who we are. Coming In is a journey, step by step, which may be shared with others, but which can be entirely an inward event, and this essay is a journey, a series of conceptual stepping stones toward our Inward Selves.

And while there are places all around the world where it isn't safe to Come Out, we can always Come In.

We are a Sixth World People

Since Stonewall Gays have been seen as a minority people in this country, like Blacks, Hispanics, Jews, and others. In my teachings I speak of us as Sixth World peoples. We're familiar with the model of the First, Second and Third Worlds. The less known Fourth World Movement (an expression I didn't make up) includes people like the Welsh, Kurds, Native Americans and other indigenous peoples whose homelands are parts of countries that don't recognize them or their autonomy. I decided to call people like Jews and Romani and others who live in diasporas Fifth World peoples.

What I mean by Sixth World People are non-biologically-related groups who are also not bound by ties to any place on the planet, but who share a common culture, history, language or ways of using language. I see the other Sixth World peoples, like Lesbians, Trans, Intersex, Non-binary, Deaf, Blind, Fat, Disabled, as our natural allies, who meet in every part of the world, and increasingly in non-physical locations, as in cyberspace.

Why We Are, Who We Are, and How We Are

If we gay men see ourselves as a tribe or a nation, we have many different clans, from leather to drag queens to daddies to twinks, from conservatives to radicals, from bisexuals to asexuals. So while we're a tribe that comes from every other tribe, a nation that comes from every other nation, a people that comes from every other people, like all Sixth Worlders, we also recognize each other wherever we go in the world and now live in a world with thriving Gay organizations and neighborhoods, which has done so much for us and the younger members of our community.

Telling Our Own Stories

Every people has a mythological foundation as well as a political and a social one. Growing up as a Jew I was well aware of the ways in which I was different from other kids, from the ones who belonged to the dominant culture. What gave me a sense of self were the stories I was told about my own people. The two companion volumes to this book are filled with stories for and about us as a Sixth World people that can ground us in our ancient past. But in the more recent past and for many of us in the present, we did not and do not know others of our own kind, and we didn't hear our own stories, for we didn't have Gay elders to tell them to us. In a sense, until recently each Gay generation had to start from scratch. But that has changed. We have Gay books, films, bookstores, magazines, archives, and if you have access to the internet, even in the most repressive places you can learn about our peoplehood and reach out to others—which is such a blessing to us and to those who follow us in their own journeys of Coming In.

It's vital for us to hear our own stories if we're going to have a viable culture and history. But stories are not the only ways in which we can own and share the richness of our lives. We often look to the famous gay men of the past for guidance and inspiration. But most of us will never be famous, and it's in the very simple moments of our day-to-day lives that our gayness can flourish. No matter who you are or where you are, especially in this time when there seems to be a return to the homophobia I thought the world was outgrowing, it's important for all of us to keep a personal archive, of letters, labeled photos, journals, and it's important for us to share them with other Gay men and to pass them on too, our lives, our work, and our spiritual legacy, for the generations that follow.

The Shadow of our People

As a long-oppressed people it is important to celebrate who we are, to take pleasure in our stories, in our successes and triumphs, and by honoring our heroes. But it's also important to look at our shadow, at the aspects of our little tribe that we do not like to acknowledge.

To start with, let's look at our high rate of addictions, the ways that we can be lookist and ageist, misogynistic, racist, and the ways that we have exalted sexual desirability at the expense of our souls. I've sat with other men, complaining about our not having gay leaders, and yet seen again and again my and our failure to support the men who are looking for leadership in our communities. I've heard myself and others complain about lack of acceptance from the dominant culture, and I've also noticed over the years that very often the most scathing reviews of gay books come from the gay press and not the straight press. All of this is part of our collective shadow, which is something that we have to face and embrace so that we can integrate and transform it, rather than be defeated by it.

Our Bodies Are Holy

I grew up in the 1950s, a time when gay men were seen as defective males, as sissies. I was taught to be ashamed of my desire for other men, and all of that combined to make me suspicious of my body and of other men's bodies. Post-Stonewall we've seen the flowering of maleness in our tribe, seen a celebration of strength and masculinity. And yet, some of us have paid a price for becoming the sorts of men we once used to hunger for. Muscles can be beautiful, but as a professional body-worker I've seen and felt the ways that they can also armor us against our feelings, against rejection. We've created a culture of looks, and this is part of our shadow, and this is something that has impacted us individually, and is something that we have to explore so that we can come back to our spiritual core without abandoning our bodies—for all of us are holy—just the way we are!

All Relationships Are Spiritual

As we claim our shadows and learn to live in our bodies rather than use them, we are ready to come into relationship with each other—as a global tribe of connected individuals, each one of us unique. It's important that we explore gay relationships from lovers and friends to family and co-workers, to neighbors and our relationships with people in stores and on the street.

I remember a day in 1972 when I was walking down the street in Berkeley with my boyfriend and took his hand, which I saw as both an act of connection and a political statement. He broke away from me and ran away so fast that I couldn't catch up with him. When I got back to our shared room in the coop we were living in he screamed at me—"You could have gotten us killed." Twice later in my life I *was* physically attacked for holding hands with another man, which I hope has never happened to you. But now, when I walk around the lake down the street from me in Oakland I see people holding hands in every possible combination, gay and straight, sis and trans and non-binary, and I rejoice. But this isn't the story everywhere, and in places where it isn't safe to come out, we can still Come In with others and move through the world in a hopefully safe way—because we do not and cannot live alone.

The next step in our journey is about families and communities. We don't live in isolation, and in our time gay men in many places can marry and have children, freely and publicly. Parenting and family life isn't for everyone, but it can enrich our lives and those of the people around us, queer and not queer. Because we are all parts of families, connected or distant or fractured. We go to school with others. We work with others. Each time I read about another queer wedding in the news, some of them of couples and some of them poly-relationships, I rejoice in the photos of the newlyweds, their families, and guests, all celebrating together. But even when that isn't possible, when we're as deeply in the closet as we can get—we're parts of communities that we can nourish and bless, that need our wise and ancient wisdom, even if they never know who we fully are or what we're sharing with them. Standing in line in the bank or the grocery store, sitting on a bus or train, never looking at or talking with anyone, in the closet or wearing a rainbow pin on our jacket, we're beaming out our wise and ancient energy and wisdom to those around us—which is needed by all of humanity if we are going to transform the way that we live here so that our species and all of life can survive and flourish.

○

- Take a long slow deep breath with me.
- Touch your body lightly and tenderly, wherever you can reach, and as you do so, touch yourself knowing that you are a wise ancient sage of the Gay Tribe who came into the world to make a difference.
- Notice the place you're sitting in.
- Feel the aliveness in your body. Feel your breath rising and falling as you sit.
- Without having to take a single step, tenderly place your hands above your beating throbbing dancing heart and Come In, sacred brother, Come in to our Holy Tribe.
- Inhale the energy of Coming In so that it spreads out to every part of your body, so that it shines out to every one of your billions of living cells, entering them and filling them with the light of your Yes, of your embrace of who and what you are.
- Wrap your arms around yourself and smile and rock your body gently from side to side, having Come In to the joyous wholeness of who you are as a Gay man.
- When you go out in the world, take this sacred energy with you, and beam it out, out to those you pass, known and unknown, for you are a wise needed Earth Sage, and wherever you go and whoever you pass—receives your shimmering blessings.

Food for the Soul: Queer Faith and Spirit

Published in *Common Ground Magazine* in April 2011

I think of myself as a gregarious recluse. I love living alone, love going for long long walks alone, love cooking for myself and going out to eat by myself—and—I have a friend I met the summer before I started kindergarten, a large web of connections I've made in the seven decades since then, and have long been involved in a number of different spiritual communities, some queer and some queer-welcoming. These parts of me dance in and around excerpts from and additions to an essay that I want to share with you now, as an invitation to explore your communal life as a man who loves men.

"The personal is political," I learned from 1960s feminists. It took me many years to understand that the personal is also spiritual, and that the spiritual is political too. The personal is also personal, and this is a review of some of my favorite local eateries for the soul, to which I hope you will stir in your own preferred flavors of spiritual nourishment.

Four decades ago, when I was newly out as a gay man, I viewed religion as "the enemy," and there are still faiths and denominations that use words from sacred texts to condemn LGBT people. For some, political action had a spirited core that was enlivening, but for others, questions of faith inspired us to search beyond the confines of the organized religions we grew up in. A number of my lesbian friends became Goddess worshippers, and some of the roots of the Radical Faerie movement are grounded in Earth-based Goddess practices as well. For others, the third and forth gender beliefs of several Native American nations and the writings of the ancient Greeks were inspiring. Each foray into faith by another spiritual scout brought back good news—that on every continent throughout time people like us had a sacred role, as shamans and healers and teachers and elders—and we can reclaim those roles and embody them once again. I was inspired and amazed twenty years ago to learn about the *six genders* discussed in traditional rabbinic texts that no one ever mentioned when I was a boy going to Hebrew School, which you can look up online.

○

- Take out your pen, pencil, pad again, and write down your answers to this question—"What are the communities that I'm a part of—families, schools, neighborhoods, workplaces, gyms, clubs, spiritual communities?"
- How welcoming are they to gay men, to all queer people?
- If they aren't welcoming, what kinds of things can you do to change that?
- If they are welcoming, what kinds of things can you do to let others know about them and to connect them to each other if they aren't already?
- How would you like to see your region, country, and the world change so that it's more welcoming, more inclusive?
- Are there things that you can do to further that?

Mentor and Mentoring

A Gay Spirit Visions Talk

I can't remember when I gave this talk at GSV. What I can remember is that I've had amazing mentors in my life, teachers who saw what was possible in me and reached out to nurture me. Over the years I've mentored 31 students writing sermons for their bat and bar mitzvahs, and I haven't counted the number of adults I've mentored in writing sermons, but each time I do I'm passing on the gifts that I was given, and this talk is an invitation for you to do the same thing.

THE WORD MENTOR COMES to us from Homer's *Odyssey*. Mentor was a good friend of Odysseus, who put him in charge of his household when he went off to fight the Trojan War. Mentor means "Wise man" in ancient Greek, and that certainly was his role in the story. But the tale is complicated because Athena, the goddess of war and peace, of art and wisdom, who was born motherless from the head of her father Zeus, on several occasions in the *Odyssey* assumes Mentor's appearance to give counsel to Odysseus and also to his son Telemachus, who has remained behind in Ithaca. And at the very end of the saga, she/he is the one who establishes peace between Odysseus and the men who presumed him dead after his long absence, who wanted to marry his wife Penelope and take over his kingdom, who he had to fight on his return.

This is something we may be able to identify with, a cross-manifesting goddess who shares her/his wisdom when it is needed. The role of mentor was named for us in the ancient tale, but the word itself entered into popular usage because of a play called *Telemaque*, written in 1669 by the French archbishop Francois Fenelon. But what is a mentor? That is what we are gathered here to explore. My good friend Don Shewey, who many of you may know from previous attendance at this conference, sent me some notes he took at a multicultural day for men that he attended several years ago in Washington DC, where James Hillman spoke about mentors.

According to Hillman, the role of a father is to protect you, but he doesn't necessarily have to see into your soul. The role of a mentor is to see into your soul, but it isn't his job to take care of you. From studies Hillman says that a mentor is generally 7 to 14 years older than his mentee, not a father figure but a man who is half a generation older. The problem arises, he suggested, when the father role and mentor role are confused, by either mentor, mentee, or both. A mentor isn't a father. What he is is a man who shares a vision with his student, and in terms of power, each of them chooses the other, one because he wants to share his experiences, the other because he wants guidance from a man who has walked a little bit further than him on the same path.

In our time together we will be exploring several different forms of mentoring, but I think it's always useful to go back to the root of what we are exploring. And the root of mentoring is in the *Odyssey*, in the Mentor found there, the wise man who is goddess-filled. I think this balance is often forgotten in the West. We speak of mentors but forget Athena, goddess of wisdom. So as we wander through our time together on this mountain, let us be men who are filled with wisdom, and let us share that wisdom with each other in ways that are loving and nurturing for all our communities.

- Take out your writing equipment again.
- If you had any mentors, write down their names and a brief description of what they shared with you and how it changed you.
- Are you, have you been, a mentor? If you have been, write down the names of your mentees, what you shared with them, and how you think it changed them.
- You are a wise gay soul, a transformational artist, needed by the world. Write down any thoughts that come to you about how you can share your gifts with the world, and come back to these notes from time to time to review and add to them.

Animal, Vegetable, and Musical

White Crane Journal July 2009

As I've explored the dances we can do of Coming Out and Coming In, I see this essay as a dancing outward from mentoring to what I'm going to call "in-touring." It's an exploration of food for the soul and an invitation to you to dance into your own inward journey of sound, vibration, aliveness. I invite you to read it slowly to yourself, perhaps out loud, and consider writing down your answers to my questions on a pad with a pen or pencil that you hold in the hand you don't usually write with, which will stimulate different parts of your brain, of your Self.

EARTH SPINS AND WOBBLES. Landmasses drift, shudder, slam into each other. Waves hiss, thunder, and crash. Wind whips through trees, whispers through grass. Rain patters, thunder rumbles, ice cracks. Rivers rush, streams babble. Animals sing, chirp, bray, hiss, bellow, howl, buzz, croak, roar. Our bodies throb, gurgle, inhale, exhale, cough, sniffle, wheeze, belch, fart. And we chatter, laugh, sob, scream, moan, wail, chant, hum, sigh, cry out in ecstasy. All of which contribute to the music we've created on our lovely damaged traveling sphere. Many years ago a disembodied friend told me that one of the reasons he likes hanging out on this planet is that more different kinds of music are played here in an hour than are played on most other planets in ten thousand years.

○

- If you were to describe yourself as a musical instrument, which one would you be? (I envision myself as an old dusky pink cello.)
- What musical instrument would best represent each of the people in your life?
- Is music purely mental for you? Do you listen to music without moving, or are you a rocker, a swayer, a dancer? Finger snapper, head bobber, foot tapper?
- Do you like to sing? Alone or with others? In the shower? In concert? What do you like to sing? Do you sing the same songs or add new ones to your repertoire? If you don't sing, why not? Did you ever? What were you told about your voice? What keeps you from singing now? If you don't sing, start. If you do sing, keep singing.
- Plato said: "When the mode of the music changes, the walls of the city shake." What was the first piece of music that shook up your walls? (Mine was Janis Ian's "Society's Child.") Do you still like it, or are you embarrassed by it now? Do you still listen to it, or do you no longer need to, because it's encoded in your DNA from playing it so many times? What else has shaken you, sent shivers up and down your receptive undulating spine?
- What music are you listening to these days? Do you listen to music at all? What are your favorite pieces of music from the past year? Several friends of mine make CDs of their annual favorites and give them out as holiday gifts. Do you? Might you? What would your choices say about you and your year? (My last year's treasure was bluegrass, "From the Windows of a Train," by Blue Highway. I listened to it over and over

again for weeks, to the great distress of my easy-listening housemate.)

- What kinds of music do you avoid, hate, wish we'd never played on this planet? What are your associations with these forms of music? Too loud, too slow, too emotional, too cold? What aspects of your life might they represent?

- Chart your coming out, love life, sex life, breaking up, marriage/s or ritual equivalents if you had any, through the music that you were listening to then. Are there common themes, issues, recording artists, musical styles in your choices? What does this tell you about yourself and your romantic/sexual/intimate life?

- Write your autobiography by listing the music you listened to in each stage of your life, or the music that describes each chapter of your life. Record these pieces of music and share them with others, perhaps on your birthday. Many of us have photos that document our lives. Why not create a document in sound of your life?

- Would you like music played at your funeral or memorial service? Record it and give copies to your dear ones. Weddings have rehearsals. Consider having a funeral rehearsal and playing these pieces of music for others. If you do this, how does it feel to hear your musical choices as if they were being played in your physical absence? Do they adequately express the you that you want others to remember, or do you need to make other choices?

- Do you play an instrument? What or which? Did you play any in the past? Why did you stop, if you did? Consider taking up an instrument again. It's one thing to listen to music, but quite another to make it. Like making love. What music can you make?

- Are there musical eras that you prefer? Are you a fan of music from particular cultures, regions, groups, composers? What does this tell you about yourself? Are these past life clues or evidence of expanded aspects of your personality?

- Recently I visited the home of a newish friend who's thirty years my junior, and was startled to discover that he has no visible music. No chance to discover, "He likes Bach and listens to a lot of Billie Holiday. We're going to be great friends." I asked about this and he said, "I download everything I listen to. I don't think I've ever been in a music store. Except for maybe when I was little, with my parents." I grew up with records, then tapes, cassettes, and now CDs that I look at, fondle, read though, and of course, listen to. Think back on the sound systems and musical devices of your life. What are your associations with them? Memories?

- Many cultures make use of medicine wheels, circles marked with the four directions. Here's the system I learned: East represents mind, morning, spring. South—emotions, afternoon, summer. West—the body, evening, autumn. North—spirit, night, winter. Often a color, animal, tree, angel, energy or quality is associated with each direction. Draw a medicine wheel. Meditate on the four directions. Next to each direction write the name of a group/performer, song/musical composition, or write/draw a musical instrument that best represents each direction for you, seeing your medicine wheel as a self-portrait in music. (This is what came up for me when I meditated: East—Bach, South—Billie Holiday, West—the Klezmatics, North—Laura Nyro.)

- Poet Wallace Stevens wrote:

   > Just as my fingers on these keys
   > Make music, so the self-same sounds
   > On my spirit make a music too.
   > Music is feeling then, not sound;

   What do you feel about yourself, your life, your journey through life, on this hissing, roaring, thundering, sighing planet? Write a song or poem that expresses who you are, your nature, your values, the way you live your life. Think of this as a musical logo for yourself. Sing/play/dance/chant/recite your composition for others. Do it at your next birthday party, and add it to your musical funeral list. Change it as you change.

- Make a musical instrument. A little jar with mung beans in it makes a fine rattle. A fat stretched-out rubber band or a big old tin can make great instruments too. Have fun. Use your new instrument to accompany you on the song you wrote for yourself, about yourself. Perform the song at your next birthday party. Record it and play it at your funeral rehearsal, and make sure a copy exists that can be played at the real thing. People have many different ideas about it, but my disembodied friend told me that it's music that makes the world go around. (At least this one.)

- And dance to it too, in whatever way works for you. In your bed, on the floor, in a chair, wheelchair, in a stream, your bathtub, out in the forest.

Sodom and Me: Queers on Fundamentalism

As a wordsmith, you know already that I like to play with sounds, with spellings. I mentioned how I used to call a group I facilitated "Kweer Torah Study," and in the essay below I dance with words again, old shy chatty fag that I am. It's also an invitation to share what we've each Come In to with our tribe. It's grounded in a story about the city of Sodom that's found in both the Jewish and Christian Bibles, and if you come from cultures that don't read it, I apologize for the ways in which Western European Christian imperialism globalized these supposedly sacred texts from the Hebrew Bible and the horrifying story of what happened at Sodom to every part of the planet.

Sodom: "a city on the shore of the Dead Sea, possibly once real but more likely mythological, destroyed by divine fire, according to the Torah, because of the depravity of its citizens." I do not like this word when used in "sodomy." Actually, I like that which is called "sodomy." But to label the sexual acts that the word covers (actually uncovers,) with a term that comes from a city mentioned in a specific sacred text, violates my belief in the separation of religion and state, although I am an active member of a particular faith.

(Note that I haven't said, "the separation of church and state." That concept, I celebrate. The expression—is part of the problem.)

Queer: "deviating from the expected or normal, strange." I don't like this word, although I use it more and more frequently. To call myself Queer is to define myself against/in distinction to/in opposition to, another group, a group that is not queer, therefore normal, normative, regular, mainstream. I want to call myself by a name that defines itself by its members, not in contrast to its non members. To call myself Queer is, for me, like calling myself a non-Muslim or a non-Christian, rather than calling myself a Jew.

Fundamental: this is a word that I like. I like it because it comes from *fundus* in Latin, which means bottom, as in buttocks or anus, (linking it back to sodomy,) what we sit on, our base, although used by extension to mean "foundational, elemental, basic." Fundamentalists believe that the words of their sacred texts are the literal words of the Divine, factual and eternally true. As a man who leads a weekly Torah Study group at his queerish synagogue, I adore reading and studying the Torah, especially with others, even though I view it as a two thousand year old propaganda text. But if I found a two thousand year old statue buried in the earth that I didn't like, I wouldn't destroy it as some people might, or try to change it by putting a fig leaf over its genitals, nor would I worship it. I'd just appreciate it as an ancient treasured work of art, which is how I feel about the Torah, as a writer myself.

As a fundamental queer Yid, (I am allowed to call myself a Yid. You are only allowed to call me one if you are too) by which I mean a man who has certain fundamental values besides a love of men's calves and butts and the back of their necks—I think that the work that lies ahead of us is not to separate ourselves from other groups of people, but to find our shared values with them. After all, Hitler could have killed all the Jews in the world, but no one could kill all the queers, until such time as might be found absolute genetic markers in fetuses which could be aborted when they appear, or 100% accurate tests for adults. We queers who are alive today could all be rounded up and eliminated, but tomorrow we'd be being born to the very people who did us in. That's part of our magic. We're woven into and out of every other nation in the world. To view the world as an "us" and "them" place is dualistic, and I am a monogamist. Oops, I mean monotheist, and I'm not comfortable with that kind of bifurcation, that kind of division.

My fundamental values emerge from my ancestral tradition, which teaches us that the world stands upon three things: Torah, divine worship, and acts of loving-kindness. This teaching comes from a section of the Talmud, *Pirke Avot*, "Chapters of the Fathers," and it seems clear to me, basic, fundamental. Torah is sacred study. Worship is aligning ourselves with the Divine, however we encounter It. (Even though fundamentalist Jews can be, when it comes to hating queers, no different from any other lovers of *fundus*, buttocks and anus. Oops, I mean, no different from any other fundamentalists.)

As for the work that lies ahead of us, one of my favorite ancient rabbis, Tarfon, is quoted in the same tractate of the Talmud, as saying, "It is not your duty to complete the work, nor are you free to desist from it." By "work," Tarfon means our spiritual work, and he saw it as an ever-flowing stream of transformation, something we all have a share in. And so do I, as something on-going, that we won't be able to resolve, but must try to resolve, nonetheless.

So what is the Rainbow Bridge that I envision, linking me with people who hate, fear, and want to destroy people like us? First of all, they would like to make the world a better place, and so would I. They believe that there shouldn't be a separation between politics and their spiritual/religious beliefs, and so do I. They say the media doesn't represent them accurately, and so do I. They think they have a special mission in the world, and so do I. They see themselves and their message as having redemptive value, and so do I. To come out is like being born again. It's a re-baptism of the soul, a way to salvation. And those are words that many of them would understand. (Well, not the fundamentalists of my own lineage. They use different metaphors. But in Judaism we say that all the Jews who ever were and ever will be were standing at Mount Sinai when God gave the Torah to our people. So maybe all the queers that ever were and ever will be were at Stonewall on that June night in 1969. We're all a part of the revolution. Oops, I mean the revelation.)

I am also a fundamentalist as a queer. I believe that we queer people are fundamentally different from other people. Just as I believe that Jews are fundamentally different from other people. (Like apples are different from kiwis, and yet are still just fruit.) Although, like a transgendered person, someone born a non-Jew can become a Jew. I am an essentialist and not a constructivist when it comes to my queer identity, although I think that there is something constructed about the particular expression of my innate queerness that's like a changing wrapper on a changeless loaf of bread. Challah. Communion wafer.

Many of the people in my family were involved in the Civil Rights Movement of the 1960's. But a few of them, as they got older, turned into racist neo-conservatives. I found that shocking, and after observing them in the context of my family, I decided that they hadn't changed, just revealed their true colors. (Is that an expression I can use in this context? When I was little I heard my relatives talk about "white people," or "Americans," using those two words synonymously. Then the Civil Rights Movement came and the color bar slid to the right, (or was it the left?) allowing people of African descent into the conversation, and ever since then Jews have been white, which we weren't before.) Yes, I discovered that the ones who had become racist were always racist. But they were covering up their racism, as minority people themselves, who'd grown up in a Christian-dominant society that still had "restricted" colleges, restaurants, hotels, businesses, where Jews and "colored" weren't welcome. They wanted to out-do their Christian neighbors, out-Christian them by loving people their neighbors hated, who were then called "Negroes" in public and all sorts of other things in whispered private. We were told again and again, with rage in their voices, by people who hated us, that our God was a jealous, angry God while their God was the God of Love. What could be more natural than to say, in the face of pogroms, gas chambers, "We'll show you who loves other people.

We'll show you who the good Christians really are. Not you so-called Christians, but Us!"

Text from my book, *Two Flutes Playing*, was turned into an hour-long choral piece for the Heartland Men's Chorus of Kansas City, Missouri, written by an award-winning Christian composer Mark Hayes. It was his Coming Out piece, a beautiful act of bravery by a man who faced the loss of his career and income. I went to the debut. Outside the theatre Fred Phelps and his followers were demonstrating, with their usual "God hates fags," signs, including one that said, "Especially fags who sing." Arriving in jacket and tie, I went up to greet the hate bearers. Almost all young women, they initially moved toward me, then away as I introduced myself as the author from whose work half of the evening's performance was taken. They began to shout their rhetoric at me. I told them I would pray for them. I meant it. Hate met with hate—where will that get us? We, who come from all other people, we whose mothers and fathers and sisters and brothers and priests and ministers and imams and rabbis may hate us—how can we hate back? If we do there is no movement forward. We only stay on the same awful treadmill we've been on as a species for thousands of years. Hence, our rainbow bridge.

○

- Make a list of all the things we have in common with people who hate us, even though they probably won't be doing the same exercise about us. Many years ago I heard gay Episcopal priest and noted author Malcolm Boyd say that we needed to reclaim the Bible from the fundamentalists, otherwise they'll keep using it against us. The most famous Jew who ever lived is quoted in Christian scripture as having said, "In my Father's house are many mansions. Were it not so, I would have told you. I go to prepare a place for you." Perhaps there was something in his essential, fundamental nature that gave Jesus insight into design and decoration.

- Let's decorate our room in the house in such a way that the queer children of those who hate us will feel welcome, when it's their time to come out, with public walkways attached to it, so that they can go back and forth, and so can we who came from there.
- Let's speak a language of loving-kindness, even when we are hated, and let's stand up for ourselves, and work to make the world a better place, even when our legs are shaking from fear and our fists are shaking with rage, justified and natural, given the way that we've been treated.
- Let's be good Christians, even if we're Jews, Muslims, Buddhists, pagans, or atheists. Let's remind those who hate us that there are many rooms in the house, and they don't have to hang out in ours, and we're not especially eager to hang out in theirs, until they redecorate it. But let's remind them of these words from Psalm 127: "Except the Eternal build the house, they labor in vain that build it."
- Einstein said that he believed in Spinoza's God, and there is only one of It, even when It's rippling out in Hindu polytheism. Believers or materialists, some Force greater than we are built this universe, and we are only temporary stewards of this tiny backwater planet, spinning on a minor arm of a medium-sized spiral galaxy. And let us all remember that the root of fundamentalism, if we dig deep for it, is love of *fundus,* butt. And we queer men of Sodom like butt too. So are we really that different from them, in the end?

The Consummate Friend

White Crane Journal October 2007

So much of how we look at gayness is focused on sexuality, by ourselves and by others. But friendship is a vital part of who we are, of how we live, and we don't always talk about it, write about, which is what I wanted to do when I wrote this story. In a very deep way my thoughts and feelings about friendship are grounded in a part of my life that I did not mention here. I started out life with my twin brother floating beside me in the womb, on my left, and I can still remember what I felt when his tiny heart throbbed, shuddered, and stopped beating, at the beginning of our second trimester. He's the consummate friend I had and lost, although from time to time he comes to visit me in spirit. (Oh. One of the twins I write about below died when we were in college, but the other twin, and Janie who I also write about, are still in my life, which is such a blessing.)

I SPENT THE FIRST years of my life in a large vertical village called an apartment house. The summer I turned five we moved to the suburbs, where I encountered a whole new kid culture, with songs and games that were very different from what I learned in the city. Friendless, shy, I watched the kid clan around me, which inhabited an area two blocks long and up and down two perpendicular streets. You could recognize anyone in that clan because they called the last large undeveloped parcel of land "the back woods," and the smaller lot around the corner "the side woods." The kids who lived as far up the street or around the corners as I was allowed to go called the side woods "the front woods," and lived too far from the back woods to be allowed to play there.

Those kids spent lots of time in shifting groups, wandering from house to house, yard to yard, woods to woods. They dared each other to break into the abandoned farmhouse on the far side of the back woods, which everyone but grownups knew was haunted. And played street games in the firefly evenings, like Ringolevio, (a word I've never seen written, so I'm not even sure how to spell it.) They all had friends, and best friends. If two boys really liked each other, even more than even being best friends, they went out in the back woods with a pin, pricked the tip of their index fingers and mixed their blood together, which made them blood brothers—for life.

Being new to the area, and coming from a kid culture where such things did not exist, it took a while before I found out about blood brothers, and then I wanted one. I was slowly getting friendly with two boys on my block, but they were already each other's blood brother. I spent more time with the twins, who by virtue of birth were already bonded. I tried to befriend some other boys in the neighborhood, but even at five they knew that I was "different." The only one who wanted to do it with me was my new friend, Janie. She had never heard of two girls doing it, or a boy and a girl, but one of us stole a pin from our mother's sewing basket, and we went out to the back woods. "You go first." "No, you." "I'll do it if you do it." In the end we spit on our fingers, mashed our saliva together, and decided that counted.

That's the only friendship ritual I know. Sadly, blood is now dangerous to share, and even if it wasn't, we live in a culture that has a wide range of rituals for dating, lovers, domestic partners, married couples, and everything in between, but views friendship as a second class affair. Occasionally I read an obituary that says, "Raul is survived by his French bulldogs and a loving circle of friends that include Tashi, Walid, Pat, and Marisa." But most often we read, "Bob is survived by his husband Marco and their Jack Russell terriers." If you go to the cemetery fifty years from now you will find Bob and Marco buried side by side. But what about Raul and his circle of friends? Will there be any monument to the way they supported each other during Walid's long journey with HIV, Pat going back to college at age fifty, Marisa's house burning down, or all the years they co-parented Tashi's three children?

It amazed me when I lived in Jerusalem to see men walking in the street arm in arm, hand in hand, both Arab and Israeli. They had a different idea of friendship than we do. This is the case in many other cultures, and I'm sure that there are places where friendships are celebrated ritually. But here, weddings cost tens of thousands of dollars, and we gay people are working hard to secure the right to legally marry for ourselves. Sadly, this emphasis on marriage perpetuates the lie that we are not whole unless we are partnered, and that if we can't be partnered we ought to at least be sexual. Times, in my singlehood, I have to stop and remind myself that I still have friends from high school, am close to two professors from college, and that two of my most beloved friends, Steve and Michael, are men I roomed with in college more than thirty years ago.

On and off for three decades I had a friend who was sometimes a lover. At a shifting point in our relationship one of us turned to the other and asked, "How do you consummate a friendship?" We can't remember who said it, but it remains a great question, impossibly koan-ish in its implications. Why do so many of us take our friendships for granted, stop calling our friends the moment we're in love, and only remember them when our relationship is in trouble or ended? Photo albums and videos from weddings, commitment ceremonies, and anniversary parties abound. How do we remember our friends? Sometimes it's only on the refrigerator. With a post card Molly sent, faded, that's been up there for years? Or the picture of you and Harold standing side by side on the beach in Maui, the time you went there with your soon-to-be ex-boyfriends, two years before he died? Do you remember your friends on Valentine's Day? Do you fill each other's houses on Passover, Pride Weekend, and Christmas? Do you tell stories about how you met your friends, the way we tell coming out stories and stories of how we met our lovers?

I mourn the lack of friendship rituals. In kindergarten I married Anne in her parents' living room. Her mother played the piano. Her little sister was the flower girl. When I was in high school boys gave girls their ID bracelets when they were going steady. I never gave mine to anyone. It was way too soon to invite another boy to the prom. But in seventh grade a girl who liked me borrowed a bracelet from a boy named Andy who lived in the next town, and told people it was mine. I don't know what teens do now, but I'm sure they do something. Tattoo their lover's name on their perineum. Get a new piercing in their honor. There are engagement rings and wedding rings. "How about necklaces for friends?" I once thought. Then I realized it could become a competition. "I have more necklaces than you!" "Yeah, but yours are plastic and look like Mardi Gras leftovers, while mine are rose quartz, turquoise, and amethyst." No, it's probably a good thing we don't have friendship tokens. Many of us will not have, by this society's standards, "successful long-term relationships." Yet we will have decades-long rich and enduring friendships that may or may not ever be celebrated. So I invite you to examine your life, to look deep into your heart for a few moments.

○

- What is the place of friendship in my life?
- How do I consummate a friendship?
- Do I recognize and celebrate my friends, or do I take them for granted?
- What rituals or ceremonies might I create to consecrate my friendships?

Into Loving Arms

White Crane Journal 2009

So much of my life, and so much of this book, is connected to the time I spent at the Gay Spirit Visions Conference, way up in the mountains of North Carolina, surrounded by trees. My first big crush in life was on the tall handsome pin oak in our back yard, and if you've read *Two Flutes Playing* you know about the idea that one of our innate roles as gay men is that we're the guardians of the trees.

When you go for a walk I invite you to not listen to music, podcasts, or talk on your phone. Instead I invite you to caress with your eyes every bush and flower that you pass, and I invite you with your tender loving fingers to lightly caress each tree that you pass. Some years ago I heard climate journalist Mark Hertsgaard speak about the imperative, as part of our work of climate healing, to plant 14 BILLION trees in the next five years. That time has passed—and the call continues, to work to reforest our world!

Here's a shout-out for the amazing book, *Guardians of the Trees: A Journey of Hope Through Healing the Planet* by my dear queer friend Dr. Kinari Webb, about her amazing healing work with people and trees in the clinic she founded in Indonesia.

Most often we think of sanctuaries as sacred places, some in nature and others created by human hands. In the Jewish tradition time has become a sanctuary, as in the Sabbath, the day of rest. Curiously, my sanctuary isn't Short Mountain, Easton Mountain, or any other faerie or gay community. It's a place called simply The Mountain, a retreat center founded 30 years ago by a group of Unitarian Universalists, high in the Smoky Mountains of North Carolina, and I've been going there each autumn for nineteen years. Perched on the top of Little Scaly Mountain, The Mountain Retreat and Learning Center has hosted the Gay Spirit Visions Conference since its inception in the fall of 1990.

From the moment we turn off the main road, I know that I am home. Car windows open, the smells of earth, rich and fertile, caress and fill me. Echoing birdcalls, cry of cicadas, the welcoming voices of loving friends—greet me and ground me in what's true—that I've come back for another reunion with the family of my soul. The values and mission of The Mountain are part of what's made it my sanctuary. Each year The Mountain offers programming on the themes of peace, justice, and sustainability, through elderhostels and youth camp, in addition to providing a haven to groups like mine. After 30 other retreat centers in the South had turned away the founders of Gay Spirit Visions—they were welcomed by The Mountain staff. Not just welcomed but thanked for coming. The staff had been praying for a year for a way to do outreach to the gay community, and the men from GSV were the answer to their prayers. Perhaps you have your own stories about sanctuary. I hope so.

Five things make The Mountain a sanctuary for me. First, the Eastern Continental Divide runs through Little Scaly Mountain. If you turn to the east and spit off the summit, your saliva will flow out to the Atlantic. Spit west and your saliva will wash its way down to the mighty Mississippi. Standing on this dividing line always reminds me of our role as men who love men. We stand on the border between male and female, matter and spirit, night and day, sacred and profane, linking, binding, uniting them through our bodies and our souls.

Second, at the bottom of The Mountain is a large beautiful labyrinth, its spiral pathways defined by stones and chunks of colored glass pressed into the earth. The labyrinth is a work of love and devotion, built by Mountain youth who painted words of inspiration on many of the stones, with the guidance and support of our GSV brothers. Walking the labyrinth is perfect for moving into your center, and I spend time there every year silently reconnecting with mine, so easily lost for most of the year, in hectic street-noisy bus-rattled San Francisco. I hope you have such a place to visit in your life.

Third, at the top of Little Scaly is a fire tower with a 360° view of Blue Valley and the surrounding mountains, hills rolling out like ocean waves toward the horizon, allowing us to gaze out at the world with more than our usual mono-focus. Each year I climb to the top of that tower five or more times a day, to watch sun and moon rise and set, watch changing weather, rolling clouds, all of which anchors me in the physical world again. On cloudless nights I plunge upward to the stars and at the same time drop deep into the dark night that's encoded in our genes, a night of star-spray and abiding holiness that reminds me of my place, small place, in the vast eternal scheme of things.

Fourth, The Mountain is my sanctuary because of the people who gather there, both my GSV brothers and The Mountain staff. I have met some of my dearest friends on the top of that mountain, which makes my annual return more a New Year than Rosh Hashanah. And the committed, devoted Mountain staff have become family as well. Each year they remind us that we are as important to them as they are to us. In an often-hostile world, such reminders are another of The Mountain's eye-moistening heart-soothing gifts.

Since childhood I have been a creature half recluse and half gadabout and being on Little Scaly nurtures both aspects of my ambivert nature. Surrounded by people I love, at any moment I can slip off and away into the trees again. Because it's the trees, lastly and most importantly, who make The Mountain my sanctuary. In *Two Flutes Playing* I wrote about the sacred role of gay men as the

Guardians of the Trees. It's my belief that in ancient times the elders of each tribe would come to men like us when they wanted to use wood from the planet's once lush forests. And we, with an innate affinity for those trees, would guide them to those who could be cut and used. Many of us spent time in the arms of trees when we were boys. Did you? And to this day, no matter where we go on the planet, if we want to meet other gay men, all that we have to do is find the nearest park. It's in sacred groves that we have always gathered, and as we remember and embody all of our sacred roles, we are able to share again our wisdom with the world.

The trees on The Mountain are not just my family, but are also geologically and botanically unique. Tenaciously clinging to the thin soil on the summit of a granite peak, those trees always inspire and strengthen me. Many of them are over four hundred years old, and they flourish in a temperate rainforest that may get as much as 90 inches of rain a year. At an elevation of 4200 feet, Little Scaly Mountain has never been logged, unlike much of the surrounding land. Strong winds blow up over the top of the mountain, and the old growth trees may be the very last Dwarf White Oak Wind Forest in the world, a bonsai collection designed by Father Earth beneath the luminous vault of Mother Sky. What potent metaphors for a spiritual pilgrim those oaks are—old growth—wind forest—which welcome me every year, and offer their dark loving arms to me each time that I return.

I have wandered alone in those woods and found solace and comfort there. The oaks know me. The rhododendrons are near kin to the ones I hid in in my childhood. Wind in those trees is the voice of blessing, whispering whispering our sacredness, sheltering and teaching me what I need to know. So I call San Francisco my home, yet my feet only skim its surface. But in the company of the standing people on The Mountain, those sacred trees, and the walking people who share its summit, staff and GSV brothers, all my true family, I feel how deeply my roots sink into that granite outcropping, making it my spiritual home, haven, and beloved sanctuary.

OUR TRIBE CHANTING

○

- Do you have a sanctuary?
- Does it have trees, and do you have tree stories to tell?
- If you don't have a sanctuary, can you conceive of having one?
- If you can conceive of having a sanctuary in your life, are you ready to take steps to find it?
- If you aren't ready, what will it take for you to remember that sanctuary is vital to our wellbeing and vital to the renewal of the world?
- Can you envision the world as one vast sanctuary?
- Is your home a mini-sanctuary and if it isn't, what would it take for you to sanctify it?
- If you agree with me that we men who love men are the natural guardians of the trees, what are you doing and what can you do to fulfill our ancient role?

Healthy Spirituality

White Crane Journal—but
I can't remember when.

This article is about a practice that's one of the most important things that I've been taught by my guides and angels, who say "Do this every day." It's what I do when I sit down to meditate, or when I decide to stand up and meditate, and it's what I do when I'm finished with my meditation, as a tool for becoming present in a world of increasing distractions. I'm sharing it with you in the hope that it will become a part of your daily practice. Again and again my guides and angels have told me—"If there's only one thing you can do to change your life and help to heal the world, this is what we invite you to do!"

There's a prayer in the traditional Jewish morning liturgy that thanks God for creating our bodies in wisdom, for creating the various openings and organs. The prayer goes on to say that if one of them should fail to function it would be difficult to exist and stand before God. Yet I think of people I've known in wheel chairs, who have not stood in years, (if ever) and a dear family member whose eighty-three year old body is failing but whose spirit is strong. No, it's hard to know what health is. And there was much talk at this summer's Gay Spirit Culture Project Summit about defining spirituality, about writing a statement on what Gay Spirituality is. But there was little agreement on thoughts or words.

Is healthy spirituality like pornography? In 1964, United States Supreme Court Justice Potter Stewart, said "I can't define pornography, but I know it when I see it." No, I'm thinking about friends of mine as they were dying of AIDS, covered with lesions, shrunken till they resembled Auschwitz survivors, men who looked like the fast-forward button had been pushed on their mortal frames—who exuded a radiance and peace I've seldom felt. And I think about my family, the Communist side, who lived with a passionate spirituality my Orthodox relatives lacked, who laughed at anyone who believed in anything sacred and would have bellowed at me if I'd used the word spiritual to describe them to their faces.

In my time I've gone to massage school, had thousands of needles stuck in me by acupuncturists, almost all of them either Chinese or Jewish. (What is this odd connection? Acupuncture, Mah Jongg, spare ribs?) I've eaten too much ghee, as prescribed by Ayurvedic practitioners, fasted, been vegan, meditated for countless hours, and read more self-help books than I can count, (even written a few,) all in a quest for spiritual health. But in the end, I've really only learned one thing that I can share with you on this subject.

Truth be told, it was much easier for me to come out as gay than it's been for me to come out as a person who speaks to angels and to disembodied entities. But I'm here with you, and you won't be too surprised if I tell you that the best thing I learned about healthy spirituality came to me from an angel, (the disembodied kind.) A paradox, that someone fleshless would give me the best advice I've yet received on healthy spirituality, but here it is—massage your body every morning.

"Massage your body every morning? Is that it?" I can hear you saying. Well, frankly, yes. That's it. As far as I and my angel friends are concerned, the path to spiritual health is that simple.

Massage your body every morning.

There, I've put it in boldface, so that it seems as if I'm saying something of substance, for substance, you see, is exactly what I'm talking about. We are eternal souls who come into the world to learn and grow, and it is only through being physical, through having substance and becoming men of substance, that we can do this. We could meditate forever, on cushions fashionable or plain. And we could pray prayers from every religion in the world, only, which of them have written prayers for men like us, for men who love other men? But when we wake, and in a silent liturgy of the flesh, tenderly touch ourselves from head to toe, as fondly as a lover, as best as we can, as far as we can reach, then we slowly ground our immortal souls in our cells. And that, an angel once told me, is the path to healthy spirituality. Try it, slowly and lovingly. Celebrate yourself through your sacred touch. If, due to age, health, ability, you cannot massage yourself, imagine that you're massaging yourself, or imagine that an angel is doing it for you. And gradually, over time, you will learn to be your body, and hear what it's trying to tell you, and you'll exist in the world with a new grace, a sweet reverence, and a glow about you that says—"This man is alive in the world!"

The Blessings of Our Elders
—Is Pressed Into Our Cells

Please take a slow deep breath with me. And look around you. And then turn your gaze within you and notice your body. How are you feeling right now? Well, or wobbly? Thirsty, hungry, satisfied? Is your belly contracted, or gurgling? Inhale deeply now and take in the smells. Of the flowers in blossom on the table behind you. The dust on the rug your feet are on that's in need of a cleaning. Notice the temperature in the room and how it touches your body—with a warm caress, a shivery contraction. Now think about your last birthday. Did you have a party? Did you go out? Were you alone? Did you get any cards in the mail, phone calls, emails, texts or other messages? From who, and how did it feel if you were remembered? And how did you feel about entering another year of life? Now take another slow deep breath, and when you are ready, please read on.

Dear you,

No matter your current age, I invite you to stop, place your hands on your beating heart, and say—

I am an embodied elder, come to help to heal the world.

Because we come from all other peoples, we queer folk (whatever you call us) have the unique ability to reach across all borders and boundaries, which gives us the amazing capacity to unite all of humanity in a way that we've never been united before. This message is at the heart of all of my books and teachings, and it's at the heart of the work I feel called by Goddess to do for the rest of my life.

When I was born (my parents liked to tell me) the nurses in the hospital wrapped me in a yellow blanket. It was 1951, when the only choices were blue and pink. My parents said the nurses wrapped me in yellow because I was such a beautiful baby, but all I heard was: yellow = chicken = scared = not a real boy. I remember sitting under a tree during recess with the other misfits in my elementary school class, two boys and a girl, watching all the other boys play baseball, all the other girls jump rope, to songs like, "Two in together, girls. How do you like the weather, girls?" (I hated the weather.)

I heard the word homosexual for the first time in seventh grade, went home and looked it up in the dictionary. "The unnatural attraction of . . . .." it began. Until then I thought I was the only boy who liked other boys, and all at once I knew I wasn't just odd—but unnatural. This was externalized when a 9th grade teacher called me a fairy in front of the class, taken up by other boys who taunted me with it for the next few weeks. But along with that feeling of being cursed—came a succession of blessings.

An English teacher (Miss not Mrs. No one was called Ms. yet) with short gray hair, mannishly dressed, singled me out by giving me special writing assignments on subjects that I loved—Greek mythology, ancient Egypt. And an art teacher invited me and three other boys to join an afterschool art class. Many years later I ran into him and his lover (in the 70s we didn't say partner or husband) in front of a Broadway theatre. I wasn't sure if he'd remember me when I went up to thank him, but he did, told me he'd recognized me as a gay boy—and created that class to support me. But fearing for his job, afraid to ever be alone with any boy in school, he invited those other boys to join too. Yellow. Scared. An outsider, outlier. And blessed by those first two elders.

I came out as gay in Berkeley during my senior year in college. My first kiss with another man happened in the basement of his parents' home in South San Francisco. Dear Richard Krawetz, long gone from AIDS. Having finally come out, I thought that at last I would fit in—but the San Francisco gay world he introduced me to was one of dance clubs, cigarettes, drinking, drugs, loud music, and having multiple sex partners, none of which appealed to me. I didn't think I could dance, and was repeatedly shamed by his friends for my monogamous inclinations. "What's wrong with you? You say you love him, but he's not your possession. You don't own him. You're so disgustingly hetero!"

One evening Richard dragged me off to his favorite club, upstairs somewhere on Polk Street. (The heart of gay San Francisco was still there and not yet in the Castro.) I stood by a wall watching him dancing with sexy other men, scared that he might hook up with one of them later. From out of the crowd an older man—by older I mean in his forties—came up to me, said, "Honey, all fags can dance," grabbed my hand, dragged me onto the dance floor, wrapped himself around me, and pressed the beat of the blasting music into my body. Soon I found myself moving as I hadn't moved since I was a boy, and when he pushed me toward Richard at the end of the song—I merged into his arms and into the next song, and I've been dancing ever since. That wonderful man, never seen again, was another elder, conveying instant embodied wisdom.

Place your hands upon your heart again and ask yourself—

Who were my elders? What did they awaken in me that I brought with me into this life? And what did they teach me?

We all belong to long chains of elders, going back to the beginning of human history, and queer or not queer, they helped to shape you to be the elder you are now, whatever your current age. If you know them and they're still embodied, thank them.

And if you don't know them, or if they're no longer embodied, thank them.

After Richard and I broke up I flew to New York to visit my father, stepmother, and her two kids for two weeks, and stayed with them for a year. Single, I explored the gay world but found myself not fitting in again, in noisy bars and clubs or at the baths, so, rather than moving to Greenwich Village, then the heart of gay New York, I got an apartment in Park Slope, Brooklyn. What was missing for me in gay life was spirituality, and that's what I found there—among goddess-worshipping lesbians. One of the two high points of my queer life was the evening I was dubbed an honorary lesbian with a very large wooden spoon, by Joan Larkin, in the company of Audre Lorde and June Jordan—noted poets—in a kitchen full of other women, all my olders and elders.

My friends were all women (several of whom are still good friends) and I had boyfriends on the side. Over the years it happened a few times that a man I had sex with for the first time would say—"You're now in the lineage of Allen Ginsberg." Or, "Oscar Wilde." Or, the one that gave me the most pleasure, bestowed by sweet wonderful poet Gerard Rizza, who died of AIDS just before his first book came out—"Walt Whitman slept with Edward Carpenter. Who slept with Gavin Arthur. Who slept with Neal Cassidy. Who slept with Allen Ginsberg. Who slept with me. As I have slept with you."

We didn't get much sleep. But those benedictions changed my life. I was in my late twenties and early thirties, a novice writer working in a bookstore, feeling inept, insecure—and knowing that the gay men into whose lineages I had been inducted were all writers—was a blessing.

Then AIDS came into our lives, and the gay world around me changed. Dying and death opened a doorway to spirituality, which many of the gay men I knew had pushed away from having experienced religious abuse growing up. And AIDS also opened that doorway because our lesbian sisters stepped forward to support us, bringing it with them in a deep abiding way that I will be forever grateful for. Another blessing.

My life in the time of AIDS was shaped by my involvement with The New York Healing Circle, where hundreds of us met several times a week to sing, dance, pray, meditate, hold each other, comfort each other, bury each other, cry together, laugh together, and celebrate the lives of those we lost. It was there that I first began to teach, under the guidance of Samuel Kirschner, one of the group leaders, who became a slightly older big brother elder to me. It was there that I shared some of my earliest gay writings, and there that I learned the blessing of finally being in a community that I fit into.

Around that time I began receiving the information that's in *Two Flutes Playing,* which was largely dictated to me by two disembodied teachers. So consider the fact that some of your elders may come to you in spirit and not in the flesh. (Thank you Yamati and Arrasu, the book's true authors, and two of my ancient gay elders.) When I had a rough draft assembled, I made four copies that I gave to four gay men. They made copies that they shared with others, one of which was given to Raven Wolfdancer, who you've met already in these pages. He invited me to the first GSV gathering, where Harry Hay blessed me as a younger elder of our tribe, as you read about earlier, a huge cone of yellow energy passing into my body. That was the second high point of my queer life. Which to this very day makes me wonder—How did those hospital nurses know, on that new spring night in 1951, that yellow was the right color for me? Yellow = different = blessed.

GSV was a primary school for becoming a mentor, an elder, and for becoming myself. My hope for you, dear one, is that if you haven't yet found your school or training program—that you'll come upon it very soon, while wandering about the world, even if the world you're wandering around in is two-dimensional, on a flat screen. There's a certain magic to that reality. For just as we come from every people and thus have the capacity to bring all of humanity together as one, for the first time in human history Zoom and other programs are able to bring us together at the same time and in the same place, while each of us is sitting somewhere else.

It's more than thirty years since Harry blessed me and I'm now in the same decade he was then. And as a now-older elder, I know that it's my embodied duty to pass on to others all that I've been blessed with, especially to younger gay/queer elders-in-training—for you will be so needed in a future world of climate horrors and the accompanying social disruption that may be worse than anything we've yet experienced in our unfolding history.

Place your hands on your heart again, dear one, whatever your current age, and ask yourself as an elder (who may be one of the oldest embodied souls on the planet)—

What wisdom did I bring with me into this current incarnation? What did I come back to do with it? And how can I do it, now and over time, as a blessing for all the world?

Several years ago I told a group of younger gay men the stories I just told you. One of them, in a monogamous relationship, didn't ask me to have to sex with him, but to initiate him into the lineages I'd been entered into—by kissing him on the lips—which I did, standing in the lobby of our synagogue.

You, who are reading these words—are an old soul. You are one of the ones the world has been waiting for. Place your hands on your heart. Feel it beating. Feel your breath. Feel your sacred body. And feel that you too are turning yellow.

Yellow = Holy = Luminous = Powerful = Blessed.

And know that I have just kissed you with these words.

Love to you,
from me!

Swimming in the Lake

The Sacred Intimate Handbook

This section of the book was written decades ago at the invitation of Joseph Kramer, and has never been in print before. In 1984, at the height of the AIDS Epidemic, Joseph founded the Body Electric School in Oakland, California as a place for gay men to ground and connect through a workshop he called "Celebrating the Body Erotic." In the face of illness and death from a terrifying disease that was/is sexually transmitted, Joseph offered hope and transformation through workshops that were linked back to the ancient tradition of the temple prostitutes around the world who offered those who joined them the experience of having sacred sex. These prostitutes were most often seen as women offering sex to men, but with my background and degree in Jewish Studies I shared with Joseph that in the Hebrew Bible these temple healers were women *and* men, called "kedeshim," which means "the holy ones." In the channeled material that was coming through me I was learning about times in our history when there were temples for men-who loved-men, where the holy ones, "sacred intimates," served our community. Our conversation inspired Joseph to create a week-long training for men who felt drawn to this role, in 1991, and he invited me to write the words that follow.

What Is a Sacred Intimate?

"Sacred Intimate" is a synonym for the word "lover." The capacity for love is built into our bodies. Generations of fear have gotten in the way of our basic programming, whether we are Gay or non-Gay, but all of us carry that programming in our DNA.

For thousands of years in the Western world, men who love men have been killed because of the way that we love. In the years since Stonewall we have made great changes in our lives. We have remembered that we are a people, with the same rights as every other people. We have remembered the importance of living in a body, and also remembered the importance and even the sanctity of sex—but we have forgotten love. Now is the time to bring love back in.

The training of the sacred intimate begins with the love that we experience in community. Resting on that foundation, it deepens into the love we share with another man. But in the journey to love we have forgotten that what we explore with a lover is a springboard to encountering the ultimate Beloved, God.

Jesus understood this. The steps in his path were part of the secret wisdom he shared with his beloved disciple. This was the path of Rumi and whether we are conscious of it or not, this is the path that we are all on. So let us remember these words of St. Francis of Assisi: "What you are looking for—is what is looking."

In the earliest days of what we call Western Civilization, there were temples for men who loved men on every shore of the Mediterranean. The men who served in those temples were forgotten by history, but information about them resides in the collective unconscious. Whenever a man loves another man, he taps into this information, which is the foundation of our knowledge about how to be a sacred intimate.

In ancient times our people worshipped a Creator who they conceptualized as the Great Mother, and worshipped an aspect of Her that we would call Father Earth. The work of the priests of our people was in teaching others how to open up the inner pathways through love, so it could flow into the world from the

Divine. This was done through song, dance, massage, trance work, prayer, meditation, and sexual intimacy.

Temples like these existed all around the Mediterranean, and they existed for thousands of years. It was only as a new priesthood emerged, one that believed that the Creator was male and was separate from Creation, that the ancient lineage of priests became suspect, dangerous, and eventually had to be destroyed. For these priests knew by experience that the Creator is always connected to Its creation, and in many different ways.

There were four orders of priests in those ancient temples, each the teachers of the order below them. The lowest order were the ones called *god-dreamers*. They had come to the temples in their youth, after having dreams in which the god came to them to tell them that this was their path. In their training as novices, they learned the beginning steps in healing, and were taught how to deepen their experiences with the Earth Father in their dreams. In addition to their own personal training, they were taught how to work with the men who came to the temples. They were healers, dream workers and lovers to the men of the community. At new moons and cross quarter days they served in the rituals that raised collective erotic energy. The last historical memories of these men come through the Bible, where they were called "kedoshim" which means "holy ones." The later prophets were continually throwing them out of the temples, for their "abominations." The word "kedoshim" is often translated as cultic prostitute or even pervert, hiding the true heritage of these priests.

The next order of sacred intimates were called the *god-touched*. These men, after several years of temple work and training as god-dreamers, were ready for the next level of initiation. At this point, they began to come together as pairs. In their personal rituals they were taught to open up to the energy of the god, so that it filled their bodies when they made love. They used this energy to re-tune men, heal them, and support them in their own spiritual journeys. Pairs of god-touched priests worked with these men through their dreams and did healing work with them. While they raised and worked with erotic energy, they were not lovers of the men they worked with, as the god-dreamers were. The men of the community that they worked with were on the next leg of their own journeys. For not all men who loved men lived in the temples, and not all god-seekers lived in the temples either.

The next level of sacred intimates were the priests called *god-opened*. These men had learned to become steady conduits of the energy from the god, which they used for healing the entire community. They were rain-makers and experts at plant fertility. They worked with animals and the energy flow of the earth itself. They served as oracles for our people, letting the god speak through them. They were also the ones who served at the altar of the god in the temple. In ancient images we find the last vestiges of this worship, where two men face each other across a tree, the tree being one of the living images of Father Earth, as a carved phallus was another.

At this level of their journey, these priests not only were taught to feel the god's energy in their bodies, they were taught to become the god for each other. At this stage in their love, each man became for his lover the doorway he had to walk through to get to Father Earth, and if you've ever called out "Oh God!" when making love, some part of you is remembering this path. Once the god became clear in and to these priests, they began their last stage in their journey, one that each man walked alone.

The highest order of priests were the men known as *god-lovers*. These priests had been trained for years to be able to open themselves up directly to encounter the god in a tangible way. This is difficult for some of us to understand. We need to remember stories from all traditions including the Bible, where God was seen walking and talking in human form. When we do this it becomes easier to understand how a god could "appear" to a man, and become his lover.

Love-making is information-exchange. At a profoundly deep level. By the time a man reached this order, he had completed the work he could do with a human lover. Each time one of these men encountered the god, he was filled with love and information for all of the people. In order to meet the god in this way, these priests learned how to elevate their own energy, shift into greatly expanded states of what we call altered consciousness. This work took years to learn. While they taught the men of the order below them, none of these priests worked with the men who lived in the outside community. Their work as god-lovers took place in the innermost shrine of the god, on sacred days, in sacred rituals.

The work of the sacred intimates is and always has been the work of conscious spiritual evolution. It is the work of creating a ladder between the spiritual and the physical worlds, a bridge that will allow us to cross back and forth between them. The Creator is love. God-orgasm is the energy that created the universe. As we deepen into love, deepen into intimacy, as we open to God and become god-lovers, we satisfy both our own destinies and fulfill the purpose we were created for, to link all worlds together in love. Doing this is the work of sacred intimates. Doing this may take a hundred lifetimes. But we are born to love and be loved. In community, supporting each other we can walk our paths to God together.

The Call to Sacred Intimates

It's hard to imagine what it was like to live in a culture and time in which sex was considered normal, natural, or even holy. It's hard to imagine a time in which there were no negative attachments to sex. But we can access the feelings that people experienced who lived in sex-positive cultures. We can do this in two ways, through the collective unconscious, and through remembering our own past lives.

No matter how far we go on our journeys in this life, no matter how deeply we journey into pleasure, I do not think that any of us can erase the earliest messages we were given about sex in our current incarnations. But we can step beyond them, and whatever work we do is helping to shape a time on this planet when sex will once again be seen as good and holy.

In those ancient times, there were always two kinds of "professional" intimates. There were sacred intimates and ordinary intimates, otherwise known as sacred prostitutes and regular prostitutes. It may be hard for us to imagine what it was like to grow up in a culture in which there were sacred prostitutes. And it may be equally hard to imagine what it was like to grow up in a culture in which the non-sacred prostitutes were not considered trashy, disgusting, sick, pathetic, or corrupt.

The job of a sacred prostitute was to connect you with the divine realm. The job of a regular prostitute was to provide you with good sex, plain and simple. Both of these jobs were considered valid career choices, although sacred prostitutes were paid more. However, their temple training was considerable, while anyone could set him or herself up as a regular prostitute. You just hung up your shingle on the nearest street corner, or crossroads. You sat on the ground, and waited for your first client. Anyone could do that. You didn't have to get licensed.

In the early days, when sex was still considered good and natural, there was no competition between the two kinds of prostitutes. There was still room in the world for Good Humor and Haagen-Dazs. Later, when sex was getting a bad name, in all sorts of different cultures, (and please remember that I am talking about the West here, because that is what we are culturally grounded in) there was a lot of competition between the two classes. The sacred prostitutes called the others sleazy. The street prostitutes accused the temple ones of having attitude. They did. The good old days were over, and what we know of as history was just at its beginning. In a few short years, the descendants of people who used to love their bodies and who considered love-making a sacrament would suddenly "discover" that sex is sinful except for the purpose of procreation. It was a hard time for all prostitutes, sacred or otherwise. Men who loved men became superfluous, and then sinners. And it's been that way ever since.

So what was it like to grow up in a culture in which you could sit down with your father and say, "Gee Dad, when I grow up, I think I want to be a sacred prostitute." And he would say, "Junior, that's great. There's a lot of room to advance. Great job security. All those connections. But I want you to finish high school first.

And mow the lawn." Maybe your Dad had visited the temples himself. In those days, there wasn't a sense that someone was Gay or straight. Everyone was considered everything, so maybe your dad remembered a cute guy he had made it with in the temple, or on the road one time. Or else, he'd probably spent time with one of the women intimates in one of the goddess temples. He was only a grain merchant himself, and saw your choice as a part of upward mobility. No, he saw it as even more than that. He saw it as a sacred job, and if he weren't more supportive, it was probably because he wasn't sure if you really had the calling for it, and if you didn't, he didn't want you to be disappointed.

Knowing your dad, you knew what he was thinking. You got real quiet for a while and sighed and looked down at the fire pit in the middle of the house. Then you said, "He started coming to me in my dreams about six months ago, Pop. At first I didn't know if it was really him, the god. I was scared. But the dream kept repeating, and a few weeks ago I went to the temple. And I told one of the priests my dream. He said the god had come to me, and if I wanted to serve him in the temple, that I should go home and see if the dream came back. It did. Last night and the night before, and the night before that."

Overjoyed, your father would hug you, ask if you had told your mother, and take out the last clay pot of wine he had been saving for a special occasion. When your mother and sisters got back from the fields, the two of you were having a good time. Your dad was the one who told them: "Guess what? The god has been coming to Junior in his dreams for months—and he never told us!" Your mother and sisters knew what that meant. It was like coming home to find out that your son or brother had been accepted by Harvard or Stanford—and they joined in the celebration.

Nothing like this goes on now. In those days, even if you said you were going to be a street prostitute, your parents would support you. Sex work was a valid vocation. Your mother would interrogate you about your corner, and make sure enough traffic went by. For the first few weeks she might pack a lunch for you. And when you got home, your sisters would want to know about all of your clients, what they wore, how much they paid you. Naturally, you would stop in the market on the way home each day to buy them a little treat, some pistachio halvah or a few fresh figs.

For a sacred prostitute, the job was not about sex, although sex was a part of it. It was about the god, the god who came to a young man in his dreams and said, "I want you!" It was the god who filled a young man with energy that allowed him to do his work. And when a client came to him at the temple, it was the presence of the god in his body that told him whether or not he could work with that man. And if he did not feel the presence he would look at the prospective client and say, "The god is not with me." The client understood. If the god was not with the priest, there was no reason to go into his room. If it were a big temple, he would go to the next priest's chamber. If it were a small temple, with one priest only, he would come back another day and hope for a different response. "Yes, today the god is with me."

And why would a client go to a sacred prostitute in those days? It wasn't just for sex. If he wanted just sex he would go to a regular prostitute. A man would go to the temple if he was troubled, if he was bursting with joy and had no one to share it with. He would go to the temple to be retuned, say after an illness, a death in his family, a birth in his family, after a battle, an accident he survived. He would come because he was on a spiritual journey, one that did not call on him to be a priest, but rather asked him to remain in the world.

For us, prayer is about the things we say. It is about words, or if it is a silent prayer, it is about our inner words. But in those days, there was no separation between mind and body, and sex for people was a kind of a prayer; a prayer said with the entire body, not just with the throat and the mouth. So if you wanted to pray to the god, you would go to the temple, to offer the prayer through your entire body, through the vehicle of being sexual with the priest who served there, whose body was open to the god, whose body was an altar upon which you offered your prayer. You could tell when you wanted to pray and when you wanted to have sex, just as we can tell when we want to have a deep conversation, and when we want to chat.

So if you think you want to be a sacred intimate, there are two points you must consider. This is the fine print on the contract.

One—Being a sacred intimate is rooted in the ancient priests who served in their temples, who were called Holy Ones. When you decide to become a sacred intimate you step into all of this history, which is stored in the collective unconscious of our species, which is stored in what Rupert Sheldrake, the biologist, author, and paranormal investigator calls the "morphogenetic field." This history will both shape your journey and color your response to this work, and other people's responses too, negative and positive. The collective unconscious remembers everything.

Two—If you decide to become a sacred intimate you will not just be making a career choice, you will be making a spiritual choice also, finding your vocation, as priests and nuns are said to do. This vocation is one that leads you toward the divine, however you think of it. This vocation is a path, a journey. It will carry you through various stages, and you need to be aware of this before you say yes to this path.

Remember, once you enter onto this sacred path, there is no turning away from it. Once you enter onto this sacred path, there is no stopping. The journey begins with other men, but it will carry you past them. A day may come, in this life or the next, when you cannot touch or be touched by everyone. When the only sacred touch for you will be that of another man on the same journey, where each of you become the god for each other. After that, further down the path, you will find yourself in a place where you are hungering for the One Lover who alone can satisfy your needs, the One Lover who you can fully satisfy, by offering Him your heart, your soul, your body.

This is the fine print. Please read it carefully before you make your final decision. The Sacred Intimate Training is an opportunity to ask yourself if this is your chosen path, the vocation of your heart. The god will come to you with contract in hand, in His own time, and yours.

The Training of a Sacred Intimate

A sacred intimate needs to know about chakras, auras, and altered states of consciousness. In the old days a youth studied for seven years before he began to lay his hands on clients. Fortunately for us in this time, we have all lived so many lives on this planet, and are so much better able to tap into the information stored in the collective unconscious, that we do not need to study for so long.

If you are called in this lifetime to be a sacred intimate, it is more than likely that you have done this work before, in at least one other life. But you do not need to remember anything from the past to be a sacred intimate. All that you need is a calling. And you do not need to study for years, all you have to do is believe that the knowledge of how to do this work is available to you—and it will be! Your work is not to study so much as it is to remember. Remembering is about peeling away the veils of spiritual numbness that we are taught to cover ourselves with in this culture.

There are many ways to pull away these veils. Meditation, prayer, body work, will all do this. So will the raising of erotic energy. Erotic energy is primal. When allowed to move freely through a body, it spirals through blockages, mental, emotional, physical and spiritual. It is the primal sea, and raising it is an inner baptism. This is not something we have been taught—the right use of erotic energy. People like Wilhelm Reich, who explored this subject, have found themselves jailed or worse, in the last few thousand years of this culture.

Raising erotic energy was part of the rituals that anthropologists often call fertility rites. To do this is one of the functions of a sacred intimate. How much better than chemical fertilizers would be a world filled with people who could grow healthy food by knowing how to use the erotic energy in their bodies. Rain making and weather shifting are also done through the use of erotic energy. If conditions on this planet become life-threatening, the more people who understand and work with the weather in an organic way, the better our chances of survival will be.

The raising of erotic energy is a major element in doing healing work. Dolphins and whales understand this. People all over the world used to understand this before we stepped far away from nature. We cannot blame ourselves for this. It was part of our journey. Blame and guilt will only add to the toxicity of the planet. No, we have to step back into a loving relationship with nature, so that this healing energy can flow freely again. Erotic energy, when raised and focused, can heal all the imbalances of life and death.

In the ancient days, the sacred prostitutes understood that beauty was a part of healing. We have been known as hairdressers and interior decorators, and have remembered this in a partial way. Now it is time for us to work with beauty again, to make it and be it and use it in our work. The healing of the planet depends on our honoring beauty, which is not about how something looks but rather about its integrity, its capacity to be in harmony with everything around it. To feel and be beautiful in this way is a major part of the training of a sacred intimate.

Clearly, the work of a sacred intimate is not concerned with sex alone. Nor with people alone. A sacred intimate knows that he is part of a great web, one that holds all of life in its strong yet delicate embrace. A sacred intimate is rooted in the past, but the work of a sacred intimate is very much concerned with the future also. By his words, his thoughts, his feelings and his actions, a sacred intimate is putting information into the collective unconscious. His work is therefore a legacy that he creates for all the future generations.

The work of a sacred intimate, in every moment of his sleeping and waking life, must be dedicated to the creation of a global culture where no one is oppressed, homeless, starving, where love is honored in all its forms, and where the human body is cherished along with the body of the planet and all the other living things that share it with us, from whales to viruses, from the bodies of the mountains to the bodies of each grain of sand. But I think you understand this.

Some Notes on Cosmology for Sacred Intimates

We are accustomed to speaking of Mother Nature or Mother Earth, and used to thinking of God as our Father. In the days when there were temples of sacred intimates, Father Earth and Mother Sky were worshipped. On a simplistic level one might say people believed the planet was literally a god and the sky was literally a goddess. The ancients did not believe that. They used earth and sky as metaphors, as symbols, as analogies for deeper cosmic ideas.

Our ancient ancestors saw the female principle as the void, the unformed, the energy that can generate matter from its own body. They saw the male principle as matter itself, the formed, the organized. So the Goddess to them was not just the sky, the heavens, and not just the Queen of Heaven. She was the eternal, fecund, Source of all life. They saw the God not just as the Earth, but as all matter, as everything physical, wherever it occurs in the universe, in fact, they saw it as life itself. And this duality they saw as One, forever changing, forever in harmony, as part of a greater Oneness that they called Ahanah.

The Goddess gave birth to life from Her own body. Gods sometimes ejaculate life into being, but most often they shape it, generally out of clay. A people who believe in a Creatrix experience no separation between Creator and Creation, as do those who believe in a sculptor God, or a God who creates by speaking things into being. A people who believe in a Creatrix also experience no separation between their own minds and bodies. For them, all that is, is holy, body and spirit.

So when I speak of Mother Sky, what I am really speaking about is a way of living in this world, a way of encountering, as men who are opened up to our own innate creativity. And if I speak of Father Earth, what I am really speaking about is a way of living in the world, one where one's own maleness is echoed in the world around us, in each other, and in all that is physical. But we need to remember that these concepts are lenses, that the Earth is not a man, the sky is not a woman. And neither are we, one or the other. We are both, and more.

In the work that we do, we may be drawing the energy of the god up into our bodies from below. And we may draw goddess energy down into our bodies from above, but in all of Space there is no up and down. All directions are one. Or, in a quotation, variations of which are attributed to various authors: "God is an intelligible sphere whose center is everywhere and whose circumference is nowhere." That everywhere is a Oneness that our ancient ancestors called Ahanah.

Rituals for Sacred Intimates

In the old days there were two sets of rituals that sacred intimates participated in, those that occurred in the outer courtyard of the temple, and those that occurred within the inner courtyard.

In the outer courtyard there were chambers in which sacred intimates were available to the community, for ritual sex and for healing. Priests worked alone and in pairs, depending on what was needed by the men who came to the temple. There were simple rituals involved in both of these practices. The visitor to the temple was expected to make an offering to the god through the priest or priests he visited, and they offered their work to him as a gift from the god. Incense was burned, a cup of wine was shared. All of this was done in the presence of the god, and if the priests did not feel his presence, the rituals could not go on.

At each full moon, the outer courtyard of the temple was opened to all of the men in the community, and the lower orders of intimates. With dance and chant, around the holy tree that represented the phallus of the Earth god, the men participated in a group erotic ritual. They drew energy up through their feet from the god, and the ritual dance ended with the men ejaculating on the tree or phallus. The energy they generated was sent outward through the tree to nurture and bless the crops, the animals, and all the people of the community. When the men returned to their homes that night, they carried some of that energy with them.

The new moon ritual was different in that the energy generated was sent down into the earth itself, without anyone ejaculating. It was sent down through the hands, down through the tree into the Earth-body of the god, as a prayer of gratitude for having been given life. The men who participated in this ritual all slept together in the courtyard of the temple, in hopes of having a dream sent to them by the god. Whatever dreams they had were considered important, and there were priests there in the morning to help interpret them.

Each year there were four great festivals that celebrated the story of the god and his human lover. The ritual year in the outer courtyard began in the spring, with the celebration of the return of the god's beloved back into the physical world. Each year, the priests of the inner temple sent one young man who was god-touched to the outer courtyard of the temple. He was seen as the god's gift to the human community, sent to bring his love and wisdom to the people. In his hands he carried the sacred fire that was used to light new fires in all the households of everyone in the community. The young man lived in the outer courtyard for several months. He was bathed and clothed and feasted by the people, as if he were a growing child. In exchange he taught them songs and dances and healing practices that he had learned in the inner court.

After a season of betrothal, the summer season was celebrated as a marriage feast of the young man to the entire community. The temple was decked with flowers and branches. The young man was carried around and around the great tree on a throne, to celebrate his being sent by the god to the people. The festival went on for seven days. During this time, as the god's gift to the people, this young man was "worshipped" by the men of the community. Whoever made love with him was seen to be especially blessed for the coming year.

The autumn festival marked the death of the god's mortal lover. Rather than being a mourning ritual, as we might think of it, this harvest was seen as a time of joy, for it celebrated the return of the young man to the god-world. The young priest returned to the inner temple at this time, with elaborate dances in which the people thanked the god for sending his beloved. Their loss became the god's gain. Later, when attitudes about death changed, when it became something to fear, this part of the festival changed its tone and did become a mourning rite. Its meaning was reversed. It became a rite of mourning of the god's loss of his mortal lover.

The winter festival was more somber, for the community experienced the loss of the god's beloved in their midst. But it was also a time of dream work, of inner work. On the inner level this was seen as a time of great rejoicing, for the god and his lover were once again in the spirit world, celebrating their reunion there. People could tap into the joy the god and his lover felt together through their inner work, and they could feel that the fire they generated was gathering enough force so that the lover could be reborn amongst the people again the following spring.

The story of Prometheus is a variation of this tale. But in the older version, the god sends his lover to the world with fire as a gift. It does not have to be stolen. But as the power of the manly love was lost to the world, the story of the god and his lover became a tale of loss and change. For example, Apollo transformed his lover Hyakinthus into a flower at his death. But we can go back to the older story, and tap into the celebration again, not the loss.

The rituals of the inner temple were not the same as the ones held in the outer temple, although they coincided with them. The rituals in the men's temple were part of the rites going on in all three sets of temples. The women who loved women had their own shrines, and the rites they performed there centered around the creation of the universe from out of the void which is the body of the divine Mother. The temple work of the men and women who love each other was about creativity and birth and sustenance in the physical world. The work of our priests was concerned with bridging the two worlds, the divine and the physical. That there were three sets of temples is not remembered by "history," just as it has tried to forget that the rites in all three sets of temples used erotic rituals to deepen the participants into altered states of consciousness.

The major ritual of the inner temple, and the start of the ritual year in the inner temple, came in winter not spring. This ritual took place in the holy place within the inner courtyard.

There, the elder priest with the rank of god-lover entered the shrine room after weeks of fasting and meditation. Through elaborate inner work, he was able to alter his body and consciousness so that the god could appear to him, initiate him, and make love with him. This ritual was performed only once a year, and it was seen as the energetic beginning of the return of the god's lover to the world. In making love to the priest, the god was felt to be seeding the physical realm with his energy, awakening it again so that it would be ready for the return of his beloved.

The spring ritual in the inner temple took place the night before the spring ritual in the outer courtyard of the temple. On this night, the priest who had been in the holy place in winter, took the two lover-priests who served at the altar in the inner courtyard with him into the holy place. He had been carrying the god's energy in his body all winter. In this ritual, as the two lover-priests stood face to face passing energy back and forth between them, he transferred the god-energy he had received into their bodies through their hands.

The two priests would sleep in the holy place, and would emerge from it the next night. In the inner courtyard of the temple a chair would be set up. On it would sit the man chosen to go out to the outer courtyard as the god's lover. The lover-priests would pass the energy they had received to him, as would all the other priests of the inner temple, ejaculating on him to put their energy into his body also. The eldest priest would kindle a new fire in the holy place, and give some of it to the young priest to carry with him to the outer courtyard. Naked, covered with semen, bearing fire, he would go out to the outer courtyard, to be bathed and cleansed by the men of the community.

The summer ritual in the inner temple was the time when the god and lover were the furthest apart in the spirit world, as the union of the god's lover with the world was being celebrated in the outer courtyard. To honor the connection between the community and the god, the lover-priests that served the altar of the inner temple celebrated a ritual there. From their dreams they would know who served which role. One would be the receptive partner in anal sex, the other the active one. The active partner would take the energy of the community into his body and pass it into the body of his lover when he came. Then the receptive partner would ejaculate on the altar of the inner courtyard, as a gift to the god of the people's love for him, and of their gratitude to him for having sent his beloved to the world. The altar in the inner courtyard was either a standing stone or a stone carved in the shape of a phallus.

The fall ritual in the inner courtyard celebrated the return of the god's lover to the god-world. Having been loved by the men of the community, the priest who had served as the god's lover in the outer courtyard would return to the inner courtyard of the temple. There, enthroned, he would be adored with hands and mouths by all the priests of the inner courtyard. The man to whom he gave the gift of his orgasm would be the one to take his place the following year as the representative of the god's lover. The one who returned from the outer courtyard would spend the night sleeping in the holy place. In the night it was felt that the god took back to himself whatever was divine in this young man. In exchange, he would give this man the gift of a power dream. This ritual was the end of the sacred year in the inner temple.

There were also full moon and new moon rituals in the inner courtyard. The rituals in the inner court were always done by paired priests, as the rituals done in the outer courtyard were done by single· priests. At the full moon, when the men in the outer courtyard were engaged in erotic dances, the priests in the inner temple would engage in physical meditation, drawing the energy of the god into their bodies, and beaming it out to the community. They did not ejaculate, but stayed in erotic connection all night.

At new moons, the priests of the inner courtyard engaged in erotic ritual in which they did ejaculate. The lovers would anoint each others' bodies with their semen. Afterwards, as the men in the outer courtyard slept, they would dance through the night, highly intricate dances, without music, that helped to draw down the god's wisdom. At dawn, they would go into the outer courtyard to work with the men of the community who had slept there, to do healing in pairs and to help to interpret their dreams.

The men of the community never entered the inner court, but priests from the inner court served daily in the outer court, as healers and sacred intimates. The elder priest of the inner court served daily in the holy place, using erotic energy to maintain the energetic connection between the god and the world. So too the lover priests who served at the altar of the inner court, used erotic energy to extend the web of connection between the god and the world, passing it further into the community.

There were temples of our people all around the Mediterranean, in Africa, Asia, and Europe. Many of these were dedicated to other gods and goddesses later on, and when the old gods were swept away, shrines to the one God were often built in the same places. Naturally these rituals changed through time, as they spread from the first temple in North Africa. Seeds of them survive in synagogue, church and mosque rituals, disguised, forgotten, and misinterpreted.

It took years to learn these rituals, years of inner and outer work. A novice would study for seven years before he was initiated as a priest who could work with the men of the community in the outer courtyard of the temple. He had to know about the physical body, all the levels of the energy bodies, he had to know about massage, herbs, dance, dream work. He had to be able to draw into his own body the energy of the god, and he had to know how to work with it for the community. It took more years of study to be able to do the work serving in the inner court, working with weather, learning the words and movement of liturgy, studying divination, erotic prayer, and how to pass this information to younger priests. It was only in old age that a man was ready to learn the work of becoming a god-lover, having mastered all the work that prepared him to meet the god.

What we can do in our time is to remember these stories of our past. When we tell them, when we listen to them, we begin to awaken the spark of god-service in our bodies, in order to raise again the fire that was lost to our people in the journey through time.

What I have shared with you is the skeleton of the rituals from the first temple of our people; in North Africa, the temple founded by Kuniata the Elder-Priest, in the time when what we call civilization was just beginning. Knowing the core of these rituals will allow you to tap into the information in the collective unconscious on the uses of erotic energy for healing and consciousness-raising. In order to do that, you need to draw the energy of the god up from the earth in an erotic way. When you do that, you connect with our past and work to create a world where the holiness of the earth is celebrated, the holiness of our bodies is celebrated, and the holiness of love.

Sacred Intimates in the Present and Future

Why this journey into the past, you may ask. I take you there for three reasons. The first is that we need to be rooted in our history, most of which has been destroyed by cultures that sought to eliminate us as a people. Second, we need to be conscious of the wisdom about our people that is stored in the collective unconscious; that was imprinted by our man-loving ancestors. Third, the sacred prostitutes in their temples were using erotic energy for transformation and healing in the last sex-positive culture in the West. Try to remember, if you can, that time. Step back for a while into the consciousness of that time. We are working to change the sex-negativity that has colored Western history for thousands of years.

But the roots of a tree are not its branches; however much they resemble each other in mirrored forms. How we functioned in our temples roots us, but there will probably never be temples again like the ones that we built in the past. There will probably never be initiated priesthoods. First, we are moving into a time when all hierarchies will be phased out on this planet. This is not the time for esoteric priesthoods, for the keeping of secrets. In our time, all secret wisdom is being shared. We have all lived enough lives on this world to have been initiated into some mystery school somewhere in the past, and we carry whatever we learned with us. We do not need to start from scratch.

Second, temples and priesthoods will probably not exist again—simply because they did already. History may seem to go in circles, and it may look like we have not learned anything from the past; but we have. So the way that we establish ourselves in the world as sacred intimates is something that we are creating here and now. The four categories of sacred intimates will continue to exist inside us, but how we arrange them in our lives is still unclear. Our rituals may reflect deep memories of the past, but we live in a different age, with different needs and different purposes. What we do with erotic energy on an endangered planet is not the same as what our ancestors did at the dawn of recorded history.

The sacred intimate training first offered by Body Electric is one of the first of its kind. Together you are cutting a path in consciousness for the men of our tribe who will follow. It is vital that you come to this gathering cleansed and in deep integrity with your vision, purpose and nature. You do not do this work for yourselves alone, but for our spiritual sons, grandsons, great grandsons. They will come to each other in their bodies long after we are gone, walking the path our ancestors created, walking beyond us on the part of the path that we are walking now.

We live in a time of transition. The patterns of the future are not clear. My disembodied friends see a renaissance of love in the future, a rebirth of committed partnerships between two men. Perhaps that will be the way our future unfolds. But there are times when I see all patterns coexisting. Some of us will be partnered, others of us will have many partners. At different times in our lives we will do different things, not necessarily in the order our ancestors did them, progressing from many lovers to one lover to become a god-lover. Perhaps we will make the same choices that the dolphins made: to be free and loving with our bodies with everyone we feel connected to, male or female. There is only one thing that our work must be built upon—Love. Love can be born in a moment and exist for ten centuries. Or it can grow over time and keep growing in new ways. Love has many faces and many names. But it is the capacity for love that makes one a sacred intimate, not the knowledge of advanced sexual techniques. So if you are a lover, a lover of yourself, a lover of men, a lover of the god in whatever way you experience him, then you have satisfied the prerequisite for being a sacred intimate.

Love is an energy that permeates the universe. Love is the energy that created the universe. Human beings were designed to be transmitter/receivers of this energy. When we are fully functional, Love fills us and is beamed out of us all the time. In the past, only occasional saints could do this. In the future, everyone will be able to do it. So if you're thinking of becoming a sacred intimate, there is one simple question to ask yourself:

"Can love enter into every part of me; my mind, my body, my emotions, my spirit?"

The answer to this question will shape your future work. If you said, "No," your deepening and healing will be into all the places of your mind, body, emotions and spirit that love has not yet entered, to cleanse and balance and awaken them to the energy of love. However long your journey is till you can say, "Yes," it will be a journey to god, and love, a journey that will honor the reason we were created in the first place, to receive love and beam it out into the physical world.

○

- Feel your feet on the floor, your body on whatever surface you're sitting on.
- Tenderly rub your hands together and then place them over your heart, and feel it throbbing.
- Connect with your breathing and feel the rise and fall, the expansion and contraction, as you inhale and exhale.
- Look around you, let your senses touch everything you see and hear and smell and feel, and know that it is holy.
- Say out loud or in a whisper or silently, "I am a sacred intimate. Alone, with others, in the midst of creation. I am holy,

I am connected, I am part of the healing of the world that comes from our people, ancient, timeless, and ever-present."

- Feel your breath, feel your body, rub your hands together and stand as you are able and sing your favorite love song, knowing that it comes to you from the Source of All That Is. And sing it back to It, tenderly, lustfully, blissfully, bless-fully, and then step back into your day.

Chanting Together in a Sacred Grove

Four Attunement Practices

We live our lives in a series of events, many of which were once sanctified by our ancestors. But over time many of us have stepped away from ritualizing those rites of passage, which has liberated us in some ways, and also de-sanctified our days.

In this final section of the book I invite you to imagine that you and we are all sitting in a sacred grove in the holy forest of your imagination. From this place I invite you to step into your ancient innate power as a member of the gay tribe, and I and our gay ancestors and gay guides invite you to do the rituals and practices that you'll find here, if, when, and as your feel called to do them, to support your spiritual growth in this time of need.

If I spiral into a story of my own, please stop and use it to spiral into one of your stories—because all of our stories are related, all of our stories are needed, all of our stories are essential, if we are going to change the way that we live here! So take a slow deep breath with me and look around at the sacred grove that holds us all together, and join me in doing the four attunement practices that follow.

OUR TRIBE CHANTING

One—a sound practice

OVER THE YEARS, THE decades, my guides have taught me a series of chants, of mantras, their syllables grounded in the very first language spoken on this planet, in Africa. Here is a simple basic two-syllable chant that you can do as part of your daily practice, when you are moving around the world, when you are feeling unbalanced and in need of connection to your Self and to the world.

- As you inhale, chant or hear within you the sound—AH.
- As you exhale, chant or hear within you the sound—TAY.
- AH in our ancestors' language means "heart, heartfulness."
- TAY in our ancestor's language means "presence, present."
- As you inhale and exhale, slowly, in and out of your nose, know that what you are saying is—"As I center myself in my heart, as a child of our Loving Heartful Creator, I am present, alive, and embodied in this sacred place.

Three visual practices

Glyph one:

There are times when we find ourselves in transition, unbalanced, in the midst of being rewired—by life, our bodies, our teachers and guides, and by the world. You are invited to copy the glyph below in your own hand, and keep it near you and look at it as you are doing the chant above, as often as you like and for as long as you like, to help to ground, align, and support you in this time of change.

FOUR ATTUNEMENT PRACTICES

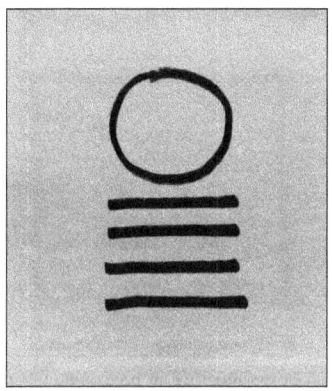

Glyph two:

When we're in the midst of transition we may feel like we're in a tunnel that will never end. But slowly, gradually, we may begin to see the light at the end of the tunnel, and the glyph below was given to us to use in just such times, to support the cellular integration of what we've been going through, when we know that our rewiring is being completed. Copy it yourself and look at it as you are doing the chant, for as long as you like and as often as you like.

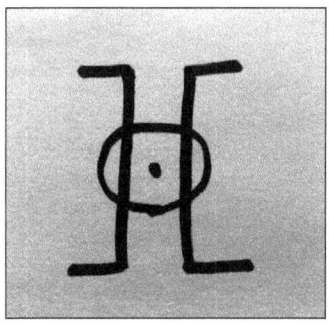

Glyph three:

This third image was given to us to look at for reorganization and balancing after times of transition, transformation, when our rewiring has been finished. And it can also be used in times of stability, solidity, and consistency as a visual focus for your continuing journey of unfoldment. Again, copy it in your own hand, and look at it while you are doing the AH TAY chant, for as long as you like and as often as you like.

A Guided Meditation for Gay Sages

I shared this meditation with the GSV community on Zoom in the spring of 2020, and I want to share it here with you as it seems to me a simple essential grounding practice to use in this time of global challenges.

Different spiritual traditions have taught different patterns of breathing to connect us with the four elements—air, water, fire, and earth. The patterns below were shared with me by my spirit guides. If you work with four other element-breaths, please use the patterns that you're familiar with and comfortable with—unless you want to explore something new.

SIT QUIETLY IN A comfortable place, look around, listen to the sounds around you, the smells, the feeling of the place that you're sitting in, and remind yourself that wherever you are is a holy place, because all places on Planet Earth are holy, even if they don't seem to be holy to us right now.

With soft loving hands, reach out and slowly and tenderly massage your body, as you can reach, from head to toes, front to back, blessing your body and thanking it for being your companion on your unfolding spiritual journey. Notice any judgments you might have about parts of your body, negative and positive, and tenderly caress them equally. My guides and angels have been telling me for decades that if there's only one thing we can do to change how we live in the world—it would be to massage ourselves for five or ten minutes once or twice a day. Or to imagine a guide or an angel massaging you.

Now turn your awareness to your breath. Feel it rising and falling in your body. Feel your spine undulating. Feel your ribcage and abdomen expanding and contracting. You don't have to do anything to slow down or change your breath. Just notice it and be present and one with it.

Now you're invited to slow down your inhalations and exhalations a little bit. Different traditions have linked the four elements to our breath in different ways. The four patterns below were given to me by my guides. As you rotate through these four different breaths feel and know that you're connecting with each of the four elements.

> Air Breath—inhale through your nose,
> and exhale through your nose
>
> Water Breath—inhale through your nose,
> and exhale out of your mouth
>
> Fire Breath—inhale through your mouth,
> and exhale out of your mouth
>
> Earth Breath—inhale through your mouth,
> and exhale out of your nose

Do each breath slowly to balance the four elements, and go through the sequence four times. If this is meaningful for you, you can play with the order and number of times you do each breath, and do them one at a time to strengthen a particular element. For example, you can do the Water Breath to be more fluid, the Earth Breath if you want to be more grounded, the Air breath to clear things out of your body, the Fire Breath if you need more energy. And if you have too much of one element, say you're spaced out from too much Air, you can do the Earth breath to ground. Feeling too wishy-washy? Do the Fire breath for a while.

Now again, feel your breath. Feel the aliveness in your body. With your eyes open or closed, can you feel any sound or vibration moving through your body, your cells? If you can, I invite you to give voice to that sound, humming it, toning, it, letting it rise and fall in your body till it fades back into silence.

Now, reach down if you can and put your hands on the floor and honor those whose ancestral land you're living on. Call them by name if you know it, and thank them. Thank them in spirit if you don't know their name, remembering that in ancient times all around the world the healers, shamans, teachers, elders were queer people like us.

Now feel the presence below us all of Father Earth and above us of Mother Sky, and draw their energies into your body and feel them glowing and merging and filling you with their holy light.

Present in our bodies, in connection with all that is around us, I invite you to feel the supporting and guiding energy of our gay ancestors in their four clans, *our* four clans.

Turn your awareness to the east, the place of mind, and feel the energy of the Scout Clan, the energy of reaching out, of exploring.

Turn your awareness to the south, the place of our emotions, and feel the energy of the Flute Player Clan, the ones who make beautiful music.

Turn your awareness to the west, the place of the body, and feel the energy of the Shaman Clan, of the healers and transformational artists of our people.

And turn your awareness now to the north, the home of spirit, and feel the energy of the Hunter Clan, the ones who seek out in the world the food for our souls.

Breathe in these energies and ask yourself—"What are our ancestors asking of me right now, and as we journey together into the future?"

Bring all of this into your holy chosen body, and lightly and tenderly massage yourself again, feeling the rise and fall of your breath in your body.

OUR TRIBE CHANTING

Now rejoice. Look around you. Stretch. Move. Look around you. Celebrate your aliveness, your power to make a difference in the world. And get up and if you feel called to do so, dance to the music of your soul that's vibrating in your body and in all of your trillions of cells.

The Awakening of our Thymus Chakra

Looking back on my amazing life, its amazements totally unexpected, the story that begins this section is one of the major spiritual experiences of my life, and the awareness that it spiraled me into is about the core of what I feel called to do, to share, to teach, for the rest of my life. As you read through this section, I invite you to open up to this core teaching, which in some ways is the most important part of this book—and I also invite you to ask yourself—"If a gigantic jigsaw puzzle were to suddenly appear before me, and if I heard the same words—what would my contribution to healing the world be as a gay elder ?"

In July of 2018 I was sitting on the living room floor meditating when a gigantic jigsaw puzzle appeared before me. It was made out of gold with darker veins of gold running through it, rather like marble, and I knew there was one piece in it for every person in the world. One piece was pushed forward and I was told—"Everyone alive now has a share in the transformation of human life upon this planet, and this is your contribution." The moment I heard that I knew that what I've been taught and been teaching about the thymus chakra is the very heart of my contribution. (What's yours?)

You may already know about chakras, and if you don't there's lot of information about them in books and online. There are seven major ones, which run from the base of the spine to the top of our head, and now, as humanity evolves, a new chakra has been awakening, midway between our heart and throat chakras, whose function is connect all of humanity in a web of joy, from body to body—for the first time in our history! I began to receive information about it from my guides and angels in the early 1980s and started sharing it with friends and students. In one workshop a student yelled at me when I began to talk about it—"You're crazy! There are only seven chakras!"

In 1987 my first book was published, *little pictures*. Not long after that I was interviewed on a cable television show with Dr. Brugh Joy, who talked about his own amazing work as a healer and energy practitioner. When I asked him about the information I'd been getting on the thymus chakra he affirmed it and told me that he calls it the mid-chest chakra, and that it's also called the high heart, secret heart, and witness area. If you go to his amazing book *Joy's Way* and look at pages 167, 168, 169, 192 and 193 you'll see some beautiful drawings of it and several other chakras too!

While the heart chakra is concerned with our capacity for intimate, personal love, the thymus chakra's function is to facilitate our capacity for joyous global connection. It is, in essence, the chakra of world peace. When all of us have activated our thymus chakra we will move in the world in a joyous way, knowing in our bodies and not just in our minds that all of us are one.

What my guides and angels told me is that it was in the years after the first atomic bombs were detonated that this chakra first began to flicker in the breasts of human beings, implanted there by our ancestors, elders, and guides, to help us rectify the horrifying consequences of that invention. Today there are people who are awakening this chakra, some consciously and others not, and increasingly I am noticing babies and little kids whose thymus chakras are awake and glowing in their upper chest.

Thymus comes from the Greek word for spirit or courage. As this chakra is opened in more and more of us, we will have both the inner strength and the outer connection to heal our world and live together in peace.

It takes between three and five years to fully activate this chakra, but once you start working with it, it will begin to unfold and function. Because this is a unique chakra, everyone may perceive it in a different way. Its color is in the blue-green family, turquoise or aqua, and rubbing the area with your hands and feeling its warmth is another way to start to awaken your thymus chakra. But the simplest way to awaken and activate it is to turn your senses inward, as you will be guided to do in the meditation that follows.

Awakening and activating your thymus chakra

Read through the directions slowly, step by step, or record the meditation so you can play it back to yourself. Give yourself ten or fifteen minutes to do it. You may want to practice this meditation in the morning, before you get out of bed, or you may prefer to do it at night, just before you fall asleep. You can do it in the shower, and it can be incorporated into your regular spiritual practice. The more often you tune into this chakra throughout the day, the more quickly it will be activated.

- Get comfortable. Relax. Close your eyes. With the tips of your fingers locate the place in your upper chest where you can feel a pair of prominent ribs jut out on either side of your sternum, a little below the notch in your clavicle. Lightly rub this area on your sternum for a while and then leave your hands there, one on top of the other, palms flat on your upper chest.

- Bring your consciousness to that area. Tune inward until you find a small warm spot of light an inch or so inside your chest. It may be a pin-prick of light, easy to skip over, much smaller than your other chakras if you work with them, midway between your heart and throat chakras. This spot is the emergence point for your new chakra.

- Place the base of your palms on your chest with your fingers pointing out from your body, a few inches apart, to further energize and help you awaken your new chakra.
- Now tune into your breath. As you inhale, draw energy up from Father Earth through the bottoms of your feet, all the way up through your body. Let your body fill with Earth energy and when it is, breathe it right into your awakening thymus chakra.
- Next, open up to Mother Sky and inhale its energy down through the top of your head till it fills your body. Then inhale it into your thymus chakra. Feel that the tiny seed of glowing blue-green light there is being fed by both blue sky and green Earth energies. Feel your thymus chakra glowing a little bit more brightly now, vibrating, coming alive as you align with it.
- When the inner light of your thymus chakra is stronger, you can beam it out into the world. Place the backs of your hands on your chest, with your palms facing outward, and send this shining light of peace out into the energy web that connects us all. You can send it to cities and countries, to communities, and to world leaders, to any areas of the planet itself that are in need of healing. See the energy of your thymus chakra beaming out to everyone in the world, shining into their own softly glowing thymus chakras so that they begin to awaken too.
- Now as you inhale feel that you can draw in thymus chakra energy from others, from the luminous aqua sphere of light that we're creating, all around the planet. Sending out, taking in—all of us joining together in a whole new way!
- To close the meditation, rub your chest over your thymus chakra again. Feel it glowing. Now, exhale this energy of peace from your thymus chakra out the bottoms of your feet into the Earth, and up through the top of your head, out to the heavens, sending peace there as well. Then withdraw your senses from that area and focus on your breath and your body for a minute or two before you get up, lightly

massaging yourself wherever you can reach, to help ground you and this energy in your body.

Continuing Steps in Working with our Thymus Chakra

We've separated ourselves from the planet and from the sacred as we evolved, in order to learn other skills. Now, having mastered those skills, it's time to reconnect with the planet and with a sense of sacredness again, in a whole new way. For thousands of years our teachers taught us that we must love each other. It's hard to love six or eight or ten billion people the way that we love our nearest and dearest. But as we awaken this new chakra we will find within ourselves the capacity to love in a new way, a way that is respectful, compassionate, and glowing with peace. For so long some of us have felt that we had to do the work of changing ourselves and the world alone. But no matter where we are and no matter our circumstances, as we awaken this chakra we will know in our bodies that we are here together, to help each other to learn and grow together.

As your newly awakening thymus chakra grows and expands, you can send out and take in thymus charka energy to and from others—when you are out walking, when you're standing in line in the bank or in a store, when you're sitting on a bus or train or stopped in your car at a red light. The Covid Pandemic is fading around us but other such diseases may follow it, and sending out this energy to others will help to strengthen all of our immune systems, for the thymus gland is a central part of that, and in the face of toxic fires around the world, and other tragic consequences of what we've done to the world, awakening this chakra and sharing its energy is part of how we can transform human life on Planet Earth and help to heal the world.

A Time to Come Out and a Time to Come In

This section was first written in 1996 and revised in 2009

Perhaps all writers do this, at different times in our lives, as perhaps all teachers do as well. Stop and ask, or stop and say, "This is my best book. This is my most important teaching." The information in the section above on the thymus chakra does feel like my most important teaching. I have no idea what I'd label as my best book. Perhaps the one after this, if there is one. And when I wander through the concepts that have come through me over the decades that I've shared with others, I am clear that it's the idea of "Coming In," the words and ideas of it, that I hold tenderly in my heart as a primary teaching, which you've read about before and which I spiral back to in this section, as another offering to you in your unfolding, in-folding, spiritual journey as a gay man in this challenging time in human history.

I WAS GAY FROM before I could speak. No one knew what that difference was, but everyone felt it. My mother and my older relatives have all told me that. And I was gay long before I ever looked at another boy. Gay before my ninth grade math teacher called me a fairy in front of the class.

As I look back at my life, I can easily see that I am gay the same way that I'm Jewish, innately, internally, gayness and Jewishness somehow wired into my body and soul, in ways that are as mysterious to me today as they were when I was 8, 11 and 16. I was gay before I found myself waiting for the Good Humor ice cream man to drive by each afternoon, a sexy high school senior saving up to go off to college. I was gay before I understood what that crush meant to anyone but me. And I would be gay if I were celibate for life.

There is much debate now among us as to whether our gayness is innate or learned, essential or constructed. I believe that both are true. That there is something inborn that's shaped by our experiences, by our culture, by history. To love another man in an American urban setting today is not the same as it was in Oscar Wilde's England, or in Plato's Greece or in any other time and place. And yet, just as a cup of water in a tall thin beaker is not the same as a cup of water in a short squat bottle, and yet is still water, I believe that there is something ineffable, liquid, changing and yet constant, that links together all men who have ever loved men.

My mother's best friend, half Irish and half Italian, got pregnant out of wedlock during the Second World War. The father of the child she gave up for adoption was Italian. Forty years later, when the son she had with her Irish-American husband died of AIDS, my mother's friend decided to search for the son she'd lost. When she found him his very first questions to her was, "Am I Italian?" He'd been raised in a Southern city by parents of English-American extraction who knew nothing about his biological parents, yet from early childhood he had loved everything Italian, food, movies, and he ended up to his adoptive parents' annoyance getting a PhD in Italian language and literature. There was something innate in him, a kind of knowing, that expressed itself through him—just as our gayness expresses itself through us, no matter how or where we're raised, although no one can tell us where it comes from or what it is. And I hope they never will. Mystery isn't something to be afraid of. It's the pathway to Divinity.

Here's an example from my own life. My parents were both heterosexual. Perhaps yours were too. And yet here we are, different. I remember back in elementary school, when television was still black-and-white, when there was a show called "Million Dollar Movie" that ran the same film three times a day, six days a week. And flipping the dial, back before remotes, when you had to get up and down to change the channel and could not be a couch potato, I came by accident upon my first Fred Astaire and Ginger Rodgers movie, "The Gay Divorcee." I had never heard any other meaning of the word "gay" in those days other than happy, but my parents had recently divorced, and I fell in love with the movie, long before I had ever heard the words, "gay sensibility," long before I had any idea that the sad sad boy I was was "gay." So I pretended to be sick and stayed at home for the rest of the week, watching the movie over and over again. I never mentioned that film to any one else. I somehow knew that normal little boys were not supposed to be home watching it. And having lived a rather sheltered life, it was only in college when I met Richard my first boyfriend that I encountered someone else who loved that film and told me that several of the characters and its creators were gay men, which I hadn't known. Over the years I discovered that there are many other men, all of them gay as far as I can tell, who love Fred and Ginger.

There are many clans in the gay nation, filled with men who grew up in tiny little towns all over the planet, loving opera, wrestling, ballet, and gourmet food shows, just as my mother's friend's son loved anything Italian. This love, this shared untaught love, is part of what it means to be gay. And this shared untaught love is a spiritual quality, innate and essential. It is a quality of being that I believe we seek to share through love and sex—that predates them in our lived experiences. It is a quality of being that we also seek to share in community, although community has sometimes been harder for us to find after ages of oppression than it has been to find sex.

You may know the song "Turn, turn, turn" written by Pete Seeger in 1959 and popularized by the Byrds in 1965. The words come from *Ecclesiastes* in the Bible:

> There is a season set for everything.
> A time for every experience under heaven.
> A time for being born and a time for dying.
> A time for planting and a time for uprooting what's been planted,
> A time for killing and a time for healing . . . .

The passage goes on to list other pairs of times, one desirable and one difficult to endure. I wish this weren't a planet of duality. I would like for there to be only times of love and planting. But I had stones cast at me, literally once, many years ago. A boyfriend and I were walking hand in hand when a group of teenagers assaulted us, hurling insults and the large broken chunks of cement and plaster from a dumpster in front of a building being renovated. I have wailed and wept and danced and lost and been torn away from loved ones. We live in a time of death and dying, a time of war, not peace. We have been hated and we have hated each other. We have fought for our rights and seen some of them legislated away. We continue to die of AIDS and we are learning how to love and work together at the same time in supportive community. So we have had our times for coming out, and now, as we move toward a new century and a new millennium—it is time for us to Come In.

Meditation

This practice will take about half an hour for you to do. You can do it alone or with others. Find a time when you know you will not be disturbed. Turn off your phone if you decide to do it indoors. If you choose to do it outside, find a place where you know you won't be interrupted.

- Stretch out in a comfortable position. Close your eyes and begin to be aware of your breathing. You may want to give yourself a gentle massage all over your body, to facilitate your awareness of your body.

- Relax and just notice your breathing now. Feel it rising and falling in your body like a wave. Let yourself rise and fall with it, and let yourself sense and imagine that you are a single wave rising up from a vast ocean.

- From before you were born you were a part of this ocean. Feel and know that in your body, in your cells. From before you were born you were a part of this ocean.

- Know that the ocean you are a part of is the spiritual ocean of gay life. Feel and sense and see and know that this ocean is timeless, ever-present, and will always sustain you as you rise up from it.

- Let your body move with the rising and falling of this gay ocean of consciousness. Allow any memories from your past, from your childhood, to rise up and connect you to this awareness of your being a part of this great luminous ocean.

- Sense and feel in your mind and in your body the characteristics of this particular ocean. Feel and know the ways that it is liquid like every other ocean. And feel and know the ways in which this gay ocean is different from all other oceans, unique unto itself, as are all the others.

- Breathe and feel again that you are part of this ocean, and yet unique yourself, connected to other oceans, to other peoples. Feel your uniqueness as a gay man, and breathe that into all of your cells. You were who you are from before you were born. Feel that and breathe with that remembering.

- Observe your life now, the way you live in the world and who you are in all of your relationships. Explore the ways in which the gay ocean carries you through life and see all the different ways in which it expresses itself through you.

- Follow the rising and falling of the wave that is yourself as it moves into the future. Sense the texture of the future that you are creating for yourself, and feel the way that the gay ocean will carry you there.
- Breathe in all these feelings and thoughts into every part of your body. Gently move now, undulate, feeling the ocean of gay life rising and falling as you inhale and exhale. Stretch and when you are ready, open your eyes. Look around you at the world. When you get up, carry the wisdom of our gay ocean with you, knowing that it will sustain you in everything you think and say and do. You are a part of it. We are all a part of it. Remembering this is the beginning of Coming In.

Action

Repeat this exercise for a few days in a row, till the oceanic awareness of our people is tingling in you, awake in you. Then find a time where you alone, or with your group if you've been doing this with others, and sit and explore how this meditation can be grounded in the world of daily life.

- Think about how you are a member of the gay tribe, and how you are unique as a member of our people. Think about all the different ways that this uniqueness has manifested itself in your thoughts and feelings, and think about ways that you could express this in the world. Will you do it through joining an environmental group, by planting flowers in the window boxes under your front windows, by playing basketball with your buddies every Sunday, by joining the Lesbian/Gay group at your church or mosque or synagogue, or by starting one if there isn't such a group.
- Create for yourself a way to step out into the world knowing that you are a part of a great nation. Do this in a way that is loving for yourself, and also realistic. Don't agree to go to

meetings every week if you hate being in groups, and don't decide to plant a huge garden by yourself if you've never done anything like that before. This meditation is here to lead you into a simple first action step. It is another way of Coming In to our nation, and then manifesting that in the world.

Community Trust

Published in *White Crane Journal*
October 2008

I've been single now for a very long time. And I've lived alone since 2016. In my dreams I'm always surrounded by groups of people, and while much of my life has been happening on Zoom for the last few years, I belong to several different spiritual communities, to an active climate change group, a deeply engaged and engaging disability community, and have a wide circle of family and friends, which are among the blessings of my life—and I hope you can say the same things about your own life.

Much of what I wrote about in *Two Flutes Playing* and *Two Hearts Dancing* is about lovers, and while I am happily single, and celibate, which comes with its own kind of sacredness, I did feel comforted by a recent tarot reading in which I was told that I haven't met my soul-mate yet—but that I'm going to! If I don't, the many social, community blessings of my life are my anchor, my source of nurturance, and it's community that I will be talking about in the section below.

WHAT DOES IT MEAN to be held in community, held and nurtured and encouraged to grow? That was something I yearned for, as a misfit boy few of the other kids wanted to play with, who ended up most afternoons by himself in the rhododendron grove in our large backyard. When I was seven or eight I started having a dream that recurred for years. It's night and I'm watching a group of men dancing together around a fire in a clearing in the woods, while I stand alone behind a tree, afraid to join them. While the waking me longed to be part of a community, every group I tried to join rejected me, offended me, or fell apart. Even my attempts to fit into the gay world failed. I don't like opera, never saw a Bette Davis movie, flunked Cruising 101 and Bathhouse Etiquette. And then in the summer of 1988, I received a short letter in the mail that changed my life, from Raven Wolfdancer! You already know that story.

As a New York Jew I found something unexpectedly familiar about the South and its outsider tradition, a kind of American cultural queerness that I identify with and have grown to love. True, the deep and painful divisions in Southern culture trouble and grieve me, but they are part of my extended family's history. And when people say that they are spiritual but not religious, I understand, although I consider myself both.

After that first conference Raven and I began to collaborate on a book about the sacred role of gay men in the world, his art inspiring my words, which evoked further images from his rich imagination. After he was murdered I assembled what we'd done into a desktop version, knowing that *Stories of Our People* would remain the unripened fruit of our friendship, which ended up in *Two Hearts Dancing* years and years later.

Much of what I know about community I learned at GSV—from faerie/pagan/Native American-influenced rituals, heart circles, and from small group discussions and long walks in the woods with friends. As a recluse by nature, with a dark teal gregarious streak, GSV taught me the truth of John Donne's words: "No man is an island, entire of itself." Oh, there was the year when Hurricane Ivan struck and we were up all night bailing water, building sandbag walls, watching cabin roofs fly off, all the while in mourning for the recent death of one of our members. Then two days later we were called upon to support the community who run the conference center as they mourned the death of the family of one of the staff members, killed in the storm.

What I know about eldering I learned at GSV, from rambling conversations with Harry Hay that began at the first conference, from our other presenters, and from nearly two decades of exchanges with the devoted men who sustain the gathering year after year. When I first arrived at Little Scaly Mountain and was wrapped up in the Southern warmth of GSV, I felt that I had finally come out from behind that tree and joined the circle of men my recurring dream had foretold, and I've felt that way ever since.

What I know about decision making I learned from being involved in a community run by consensus, a slow and marvelous process that unfailingly creates a perfect conference every year. Little Scaly Mountain is also home to a lush communities of rhododendrons, to which I always retreat for some time of meditation, comforting me as they did when I was small. And there is also a family of ancient dwarf oaks, the descendants of survivors from the last Ice Age, whose glaciers slowly advanced from the north but stopped just before they reached Little Scaly. I've learned so much from that community of trees, which seeded the East Coast woodlands after the last of the ice receded, and it's those wise ancient oaks who are the inspiration for this practice.

○

- Take a blank 8 ½ by 11 sheet of what we used to call typing paper, that's now called copy paper or printer paper. On this blank sheet draw the outline of a tree with a nice broad trunk and roots and branches spreading out above and below, mirroring each other.
- This tree is a map of your communities. Start at the roots of your tree and write in along them the names of the communities, good and bad, nurturing and stifling, that you belonged to in the past: family, religious groups, schools, glee club, drama club, track team, summer camps, out crowd, etc.

- On the edge of the roots write in the names of the groups you didn't belong to but longed to be a part of. And beyond those groups, near the bottom of the page, write in the names of the groups you didn't belong to and didn't want to belong to.
- Now move up to the trunk of your tree and write in, right in the center: ME. Sometimes we think of ourselves as individuals, but as Whitman said, "I am a large, I contain multitudes," so I invite you to include the community of yourself/yourselves, as part of your tree. Above and below yourself write in the names of the communities you're most intimately connected with, family, friends, spiritual/political/educational groups you belong to, your coworkers, all the communities you are involved with on a daily basis. These can be cyber communities, and please keep in mind that your communities may not just be people. Pets, flocks, herds, parks, gardens, nature spirits, disembodied friends and angels also belong on the list of your most intimate communities.
- Next go up to your tree's branches, and write in the names of communities you are less involved in, that you connect with from time to time. The people from the annual yoga retreat you see once a year. Your dentist, doctor and the people in their offices, the people in the salon where you get your hair done, and the workers in your favorite health food store. And don't forget the family around the corner who you run into at the park three or four times a year, whose names you don't even know but who you always enjoy seeing, watching their kids grow. And your never-married Aunt Minnie, who you visit every few years, the one who tells you the truth about your family that your parents never would.
- At the very tips of your tree's branches, on different limbs, write in: the names of communities and groups you want to belong to, groups you don't know how to get into, and groups you suspect wouldn't want you that you still feel drawn to. People with homes in three different locations, close friends of your favorite celebrity, enlightened beings who have burned away all of their karma.

- Out beyond the branches, near the edge of the page, write the names of communities you don't belong to and don't want to belong to. Born again Wiccans, Bio-diesel fundamentalists, unrepentant Republicans, people who eat steak, may all be on your list.
- When you are done, draw a box around the tree at the edges of the page. This rectangular box represents All of Life on Earth. It includes the communities you belong to and the ones you don't belong to. It includes all the groups you don't ever want to belong to, that wouldn't want you anyway, all of which we are still connected to, and must learn to live with, for we share the same small orbiting sphere and the same destiny—to live together, or die together.

This tree is a portrait of the communities of your life. It may take you several days or longer to create it. I spent over a week working on mine. I kept remembering communities I'd belonged to. That meditation group in the early 80s, those friends I used to go bird watching with, the food coop I went to with my first boyfriend in Berkeley, that class for post bar mitzvah nerds our rabbi taught in his study.

Tape your tree up over your night table, on your refrigerator door, on the wall across from your toilet. Put it somewhere where you can meditate upon it, feel your way into it, and see and sense how this tree of yours is connected to the trees of everyone else in the world.

Make a copy of your tree and fold it up and put it in your wallet. Slip it in your desk drawer at work and sneak looks at it during the day, when you're supposed to be doing something else. Ask yourself how this tree appears to you. Is it bottom or top heavy? Is your trunk bare or filled with loved ones? How would you like this tree to look? What would you like to see upon it? Out in the world are there other communities that you think could feed your soul, so that in a year's time you can draw a new tree, one that mirrors back to you your connection to others who hold you and nurture you and encourage you to grow?

Eldering and Youngering

We live in a youth-oriented society. How much money do we spend each year on products and procedures to keep us looking younger? Not too long ago a neighbor down the street, on finding out that I'm 73, said to me with amazement on his lovely face, "Oh my God! I thought that you were fifty-six!" I cracked up laughing, flattered, grateful, and a little bit pouty. I mostly like being an elder, continue to feel honored by Harry Hay blessing me all those years ago as a younger older of our tribe, and feel blessed to have lived long enough to be in the same decade of life as he was when he blessed me. I've been bald for way longer than I had hair, and can still go for five hour walks, but there are days when I catch a glimpse of my old man face in a mirror and the wild little boy inside me shouts—"NO!"

We are like trees. Every year of life is another ring within us. And at the same time, the outer bark is getting older and older. The comic writing below is an invitation to own who we are and not who our capitalist society wants us to be.

You're not happy about your appearance, and are considering plastic surgery. Some of your friends are for it, others against.

Finally you decide that you don't believe in reincarnation, you only have one life to live, and you want your outsides to match your insides. Anxious, eager, you go under the knife during the long Labor Day weekend, and take a week off on the other side. "Oh my God!" your coworkers say when you get back. "You look fantastic. At least ten years older!" You've been coloring your hair gray for a while, but the new wrinkles around your eyes, the added creases in your cheeks, and the enhanced wattle beneath your chin are so sexy that you get cruised on the street like you've never been cruised before. "It was worth it," you tell your smiling best friends over dinner. "I wish I'd done this a long time ago."

Whatever age you are right now, take off all your clothes, and look into a mirror—in a world where not Youth but Age = Beauty. Frankly, a hard stomach is only half-formed. Your pecs won't be ripe for anyone to sink their teeth into until they've drooped. And if the flesh on the bottom of your arms doesn't sway when you swing them, your beautiful elderhood will have to be grown into. Get used to being ignored when you enter rooms filled with handsome older men, bald and gray and magnificent. Accept the fact that you'll be walking down the street feeling invisible for a while longer. You're going to age like fine wine, slowly, but doing the following things may augment your inner fermentation and prepare you for your own luscious future.

○

- An elder is like a mighty tree, with a ring for every year of his life contained within his gorgeous aging body. As you move through the world, pay increasing attention to older men, and allow yourself to feel and know that you are part of a tribal chain, going back through history, linking elders and youngers, a chain which helps to hold the world together.

- Whatever your age is, find a mentor, a man at least ten years older than you are. Spend time with your mentor on a regular basis. Take him out to lunch in lovely places, buy him small things that will enhance his physicality, and treat him the way that you would like to be treated when you're his age. Bask in his beauty and wisdom, and be open to his guidance.

- If your mentor has no heirs, no children, show him by your integrity and devotion that you are a worthy recipient of anything that documents his life as a man who loves men, such as photo albums and old love letters. These you will cherish, learn from, and one day pass on to your own spiritual son or sons, along with material from your own life, so that the tribe of men who love men doesn't have to reinvent itself, over and over again, in each generation.

- If you laughed your way through this piece, because you don't believe a word of it, look at yourself in the mirror again. Stare into your eyes and know that if you're lucky and live long enough, your butt will droop, your belly will hang, hair will vanish from some places and appear in others—all of which will herald your mature perfection in physical form. And if you think or know that you will not live to have an older body, remember that anyone who stands near the doorway out of this world ages and ripens into wisdom and grace no matter what his age is, and becomes an elder for all the world to honor.

- And if you still don't believe that when you are older you will be beautiful, cherished, admired, and turned to for guidance, ask yourself why not, and ask yourself what it will mean to you to cultivate these ideas and invite your own inner elderhood to blossom within you, day by day.

Awakening the Elder Within

Many years ago I spent one afternoon with a week with a beloved aunt who was slowly declining into dementia. As her journey deepened, to the dismay of her kids and grandkids, she would tell the same stories, over and over and over again. But I'm a writer and storyteller, and I loved it! I loved when she'd tell me for the thirty-seventh time what it was like when she and her family came here from Russia in steerage, and when she told me for the hundred-and-seventh time how she met my uncle getting off the Staten Island Ferry. I came to a deep understanding that I've never heard a single medical professional share—that what we call dementia, Alzheimer's, is actually an evolutionary gift that evolved back in the days before there was writing of any kind, when very few people lived to be very old—when those who did needed to tell and retell our ancestral stories to the younger members of their tribe, in order to preserve our rich history. Thank you Auntie Manya for this teaching, and for all of the amazing stories you shared with me, that helped to prepare me for my own life's work as an elder!

NOT TOO LONG AGO Inner Child work was popular. We were invited to awaken, not the actual historical child we were, who suffered and was wounded, but the Magical Child, the Divine Child, the archetype of pure creative joy and wonder. "It's never to late to have a happy childhood," a tee shirt of the time read. Inner Child Work was seen as a doorway to that happy time.

There is another aspect to our Inner Work, a balance to our Inner Child work. I think of it as Awakening the Elder Within, and this chapter branches out from the one above on Eldering and Youngering. For many of us it's easier to connect with the Inner Child than the Inner Elder. All of us were children, and through that part of ourselves we can access the Magical Child we probably didn't get to be. Some of us, however, are not yet old in years, and many of us will not live long enough in these bodies to become old in years. But just as there is a Child within us, always, no matter how old we become, there is also an Elder within us, no matter how young we are.

Once, becoming an elder was the goal of a life's journey. But our culture is focused on youth. We are encouraged to color our hair, banish our wrinkles, and fear our sagging flesh, as if old age were a crime. Given this collective fear of getting older, we are not encouraged to celebrate the passage of time, which keeps us from tapping into the sane, sober, serene wisdom of our Inner Elderhood. But it's this very energy that so many of us are in need of, as a balance to the fast paced lives we live, and as a balance to the self-absorbed creative fire that comes from our Inner Child. Even at birth we have an Inner Elder, a part of us that lives in and for community wholeness, the community of self and the community of the world.

In spite of any fear or distaste for getting older, your Inner Elder may surface from time to time, without you recognizing it. I still remember my first Inner Elder moment. When my older cousin Michael turned five our grandmother had his baby shoes bronzed, which was a popular thing to do in the 1950's, at least where I lived. Michael's shoes were mounted on marble and turned into bookends, but I had thrown one of my baby shoes out the window of our New York City apartment, and so, with only one shoe left, bookends were out of the question. Still, when I turned five, our grandmother sat me down with a catalog. We looked at pictures of baby shoes turned into inkwells, nightlights, desk lamps, and paperweights. But as we flipped through the pages, a Presence, a Clarity, a Depth of Wisdom and Certainty rose up inside me. I turned to my grandmother as if I were a man of advanced years, who knows from experience what he likes and what he wants, and said in a voice that startled both of us, something very like, "I don't want it turned into anything. I just want it plain." And, being a wise and respectful grandmother, she didn't try to talk me out of my decision, and had my baby shoe bronzed, just as it was. It sits on the dresser by my bed, and to this day, almost seventy year later, when I look at my baby shoe I can still feel the presence of my Inner Elder making itself known for the first time through the little boy that I was.

At different times throughout my life this Voice has guided me, moved me, appeared in my dreams. Perhaps you too have had Inner Elder moments, that you haven't identified as such, that you can go back to and deepen into. Just as it's never too late to have a happy childhood, it's never too early to have a happy elderhood. What follows is a short meditation that may help you connect with your own Inner Elder. Many meditation traditions encourage us to sit on the ground, cross-legged. But for this meditation, I suggest that you sit in a chair, with your feet on the floor. And we are usually encouraged to sit erect, with our spines straight. But for this exercise I suggest that you slump over a bit and settle into yourself, like a very ripe peach that's lost some of its firmness, but none of its sweetness.

○

- Relax, let go of any tension you feel in your body. Settle into your seat and feel your breath slowly rising and falling.

- Let go of any thoughts of the day, and allow yourself to be present, like an old dog or cat, basking in a sunny patch of warmth on the ground.

- Notice any fears or negative thoughts you may have about aging, illness, or your death. Acknowledge them and let go of them for right now.

- Lightly massage your hands, and feel within them the wisdom that you possess, wisdom that is far greater than your chronological years. Now bring your hands to your face and lightly caress it. As you do this, mull over your life and think of situations when that timeless wisdom manifested itself in your thoughts or actions, in times when you understood things you weren't old enough to understand, or made decisions with an uncanny sense of rightness that came from deep within you.

- Focus on one of these events. Summon up in your mind all the details you can, of place, time, mood. Recreate in your body the same feelings you felt then, when timeless wisdom filled you.

- As you continue to breathe, deepen further into that time, that feeling, that state of certain knowing. As you do this, a soft light will begin to rise up in the very core of your body, underneath all of your thoughts and feelings. This emergent light is the inward presence of your Inner Elder.

- Breathe with this light. Allow it to rise and slowly fill your entire body, from head to toe. Bask in this light and become it, no matter how young you are. Become your Inner Elder, wise, strong, and loving.

- Notice your chair again, your elder's chair. Settle yourself into it, glowing with all the wisdom of your Inner Elderhood. This elder is the link between you and your soul. Become it. Be it. Be the Elder you have always been, were always meant to be, no matter how old you are right now.

- You can come back to this state whenever you want to tap into your Inner Elderhood. But for now, caress your beautiful elder face, rub your wise, strong, and creative elder hands. Bring your awareness back to the room, the moment. Breathe. Hum. Rejoice in all that you are, all that you do, all that you bring to the world.

Aligning with Your Sacred Earth Sages

As we come to the end of the book, I want to spiral back again to thoughts, ideas, and concepts that I've mentioned before—all in the same spirit—of supporting you in your unfolding journey as a Gay Earth Sage. In earlier sections I've spoken about our guides, and here I'm going to expand on those ideas with a grounded and grounding practice for your to explore. I'm sharing this with you for two reasons. First, because my own guides wanted me to include it here as a simple practice for you to do, as an invitation to narrow the distance between what I do and share and what you can and will do and share, for our tribe and with the world, in this increasingly challenging time. So take a breath. Massage your sacred chosen body. And open up to all the Earth Wisdom that is waiting to flow through you, Wisdom our society does not invite us to open up to. Luminous wisdom that surrounds us at every moment.

○

- Sitting quietly, preparing to be an embodied agent for healing and change all over the world, lightly massage yourself from head to toe, blessing your sacred chosen body with your loving hands.

- Open up to the energies flowing up through you from Father Earth and down through you from Mother Sky, flowing into and through you, swirling, spiraling, glowing, blending into a radiant wholeness pouring into all of your trillions of cells.
- Place your hands on your upper chest and connect with your glowing thymus chakra, and feel that you are connected to all the members of our tribe and to all of humanity.
- Feel your breath, your body, your connections to the world, and know that you are a sacred elder, here to make a difference in the world.
- Life is grounded in earth. See, feel, and imagine on the ground to the left of where you sit—a small stone. It could be an ordinary beach stone, a rock you picked up while gardening in your backyard, or it could be a quartz crystal, a polished piece of carnelian, a raw chunk of larimar. See and feel it in your mind's eye, with all of your inner senses. You do not need a real stone. Just an energetic one.
- Now turn your inward gaze directly in front of you and feel growing up from the soil of your mind's far-seeing eye, some kind of plant. It could be a tiny mushroom, a blossoming flower, a swaying bush, a hearty tree. It could be tiny or towering above you, its branches spread out over you, come to deepen your connection to the world of all growing things
- Now, turn your attention to your right and feel beside you some kind of living creature. It could be a fluttering butterfly, a turtle, a bird, a dog, a bear, an elephant, a breaching whale. Feel it beside you, in all of its animal wisdom and ancient power, and know that it has come to support you in your own sacred animal body, that it is here to share its embodied experience, medicine, and its animal wisdom with you.
- Lastly, shift your inner senses toward your back, and feel that sitting right behind you is another human being. Sense the

way that it, that he, supports you. Because, sitting right behind you is one of the gay/queer members of The Council of Earth who has been with you since before you were born, holding you, guiding you, loving you, always. Please sense this wise ancient teacher sitting behind you now, supporting and nourishing you through their own beingness.

- Sit quietly feeling all of your wisdom council gathered all around you. These are the beings who support you, guide you, and bless you in your sacred work, now and always.
- Breathe with them. Feel safe and empowered and embodied in the circle they've created around, with, and for you. And know that from now on, whenever you sit or stand to chant or meditate or pray, that you can call to them, feel them, know that you are held and loved by them.
- Know that each time you sit and open up to them, that you may find a different rock, tree, animal, person sitting with you.
- Sit, feel, breathe, open, move, and when you are ready to come back to the world of daily life, thank your guides for being with you, and know that you carry their love and wisdom with you as you step into your day. And consider doing this work with others, in this time of challenges when all of us are needed to be the Earth Healers we all are.

Thoughts for a Gathering

each of us has lived many lifetimes before
our purpose in gathering together is not to follow any one path
but to share our collective wisdom while we still have a chance

in this time of global heating and spreading fires
rather than ever again building sacred fires
we will gather around a sacred stone
easily found and then returned to the earth

let us begin each gathering in deep embodied silence
looking around the circle and bowing to the elder in each one of us
no matter their current chronological age

the role of a leader or leaders is not to further their own wisdom
but to support and guide the group in creating a new mosaic
from pieces of what everyone has brought with them

let us remember that brevity is our most holy gift to each other
not sharing our stories for we no longer have time to do that
but rather sharing the seeds of our gathered wisdom

more important than having the right answer
is knowing how to ask the right questions
when someone shares we will ask at least three questions
before we share what we have brought with us

in silence we end our gatherings as we begin them
feeling the presence of everyone in the circle
as an equal and an elder and a transformational artist
all of us bowing to each other in our collective unity
as members of one family and one tribe and one species
all living together on one damaged world

Tayarti's Peace-Light Prayer

THANK YOU FOR WANDERING through this forest-book with me, whether the one you read was made from paper, from trees, or not. And thank you for sharing it with others, if you did. And thank you for coming to this section with me. With me and with our Elders, with the guides who shaped and largely wrote it through me. For you, for us, for all of our tribe. Now and in the past, and down through time.

Take a moment now to feel your body, your breath, and notice where you're sitting, the holy place you find yourself in, because all places are holy, everywhere.

Take a moment now, as you come to the end of this book, to feel your sacred role as a wise soul who chose to come back into this world to make a difference—and ask yourself now—"What are my next steps?" And write them down. And keep adding to them as your continue on your sacred journey.

The short prayer below was given to me by an ancient gay teacher named Tayarti who's a central character in *Two Flutes Playing*, and who came to visit me for a short time in 1981 and 1982. The English version of his prayer appears at the end of *Two Flutes Playing*, but the original words weren't given to me till later on. I'm including them here, at the end of this section of ritual, as a way of wrapping things up and spiraling us back to The Source—the Creator of All That Is—our Infinite Mother.

OUR TRIBE CHANTING

As you read them, feel that you, that we, we holy men who love men, are gathered together in a sacred grove, surrounded by magisterial trees. A sacred grove that could be—someone's living room, basement, backyard—a classroom, meeting hall, house of prayer—a cave, a beach, a bar, a gym, a restaurant, the top of a mountain.

Mother of all, open our hearts.	Neswat talmaneshi, salati aymanata.
Mother of all, fill us with wisdom.	Neswat talmaneshi, susudah ba-yumal.
May our love be a fountain that cleanses the world.	Sukanti intaki tay humalti ibenna.
May all be washed clean, be washed pure, be made whole again.	Sumitra malendra tiparti malakka tisruda avendra.
Through our love, which is Your nature.	Chira kanti insu maliah.
Through our love, which is Your name.	Chira kanti insu tariah.
Mother of all, a thousand blessings.	Neswat talmaneshi inutu prudiat.
Peace peace peace peace peace peace forever.	Sanesh sanesh sanesh sanesh sanesh sanesh hitalomi.

Coda: Singing in the Arms of the Trees

Up above my laptop, as I look out the sliding door to my balcony—the flat gray roof of the building next door, a few trees, the Cathedral of Christ the Light, a sliver of Lake Merritt, and the tall buildings of downtown Oakland, angled in front of blue sky and a few white drifting clouds. My home—the Land of Oaks. My very first crush—the tall handsome pin oak in the backyard of my childhood home.

I didn't plan to write this book, as you know. And now, as it's coming to an end, I'm sitting and thinking and feeling and looking and listening and remembering and smiling. I'm smiling at you, my tribal brothers, and I'm smiling at the unexpected magic of what happened to me after I put together the sections of this book.

I was sitting and meditating one morning when I felt a shift of energy around me. I didn't deepen into what was happening; I just wrote about it in notebook 166 of my journal, which I began keeping in 1971. The next day—April 20th—when I sat down to meditate, I felt a warm wise loving presence sitting across from me. As I slowly opened up I could feel the syllables of his name energetically coming toward me, and being me, I wrote down CHURAH in my journal and began to take dictation from him:

CODA: SINGING IN THE ARMS OF THE TREES

> Now you open up to me, your new/old guide. Sit quietly and feel me for a while, and then come back so I can speak.

That I did, and then he went on.

> I was Tayarti's partner and heir. In the pattern of the time I was younger, his third younger lover, the first two having died before him, for he lived for a very long time. We met in my village in what is called France now, and immediately connected, joined together, and I traveled with him, continued to teach after he died, and chose a younger partner for myself after he died—you—as you may partially remember having briefly remembered before, many years ago. So you are in his lineage, you who were called Nashan back then. You were born in a village in now northern Italy, which much later your biological ancestors came to from the Middle East, and you were my own younger lover and went on to succeed me. And your younger lover and heir was a lovely handsome man named Nahali, and this Nahali went on to become, much later, the young man who changed your life and died too soon—Erick Faigin.

As I heard and felt his words, I did remember way back in the 1980s having momentary flashes as I took dictation for what became *Two Flutes Playing* that I had in some way been part of that ancient story. And to this day I think of Erick Faigin, my freshman college roommate, who started me on my spiritual journey before I even had those words to describe it, beginning in the fall of 1969 at the University of California at Santa Barbara, giving me books to read, taking me to lectures and classes and talking about spirituality while we ate, on our long walks, and back in our dorm room. I remember a night, near the end of the school year, talking as we always did, in our parallel beds, to the sound of waves breaking in the distance, when he paused and then said something very like—"Sometimes. Perhaps. Maybe. Just a little. It's possible. That I might. Be attracted. To. Other. Boys." No one had ever come out to me before. But amazed, in response to his words, I was able to stammer out, "Me too."

CODA: SINGING IN THE ARMS OF THE TREES

Erick started me on my spiritual journey, and this book and all my books exist because of him, and my life as it is exists because of him. Thank you my sacred brother, who died three weeks after our freshman years ended, accidentally electrocuted at your summer job in an aviation factory—with a book in your hand. Fifty four years later, Erick, I still look at a picture of you every day!

A song in the trees. A song of joy and sorrow. Erick and a new guide, Churah, whose presence I feel whenever I sit quietly, and who continues to talk with me and dictate to me. His coming to me as much of a joyous surprise as were Erick's words.

Erick. And Churah. Who in subsequent dictations went on to tell me about other dear ones in this life who I knew when I was his lover. And then, at 5:14 on April 23rd, awake in the night and opening up to him, notebook on my desk, pen in hand, the curtain over the desk in my bedroom pulled back so that I could gaze out into the Land of Oaks at night, he said and I recorded:

> Sitting here and looking at the Cathedral of Christ the Light, in one of his past lives Yeshua was a man named Tarug, a student of Tayarti, and in another past life he was Leah bat Shmuel, one of the students of the prophet Deborah in her training school for women. So sit. Feel him as you look out at one of his many shrines, two of the past lives he was anchored in—one gay and one as a woman. And write about that, about his roots, something very few if any have done before. A new "revelation" coming through, my dear.
>
> Enough for now. Much to sit in and hold, get used to, and be holding, your holy circle of blessing. In the midst of God's rich universe of unfoldingness. Yes.

Wow! That was so *not* what I was expecting. Not that I was expecting anything in particular. Some years ago one of my guides told me about the school for training women to be prophets that Deborah had started, long lost from history, and told me that I had once been a student in it. And now I'm sitting here at my desk, looking out at the Cathedral of Christ/Yeshua/Jesus, who had once been Turag and then Leah, smiling.

CODA: SINGING IN THE ARMS OF THE TREES

It's a bleak gray day as I'm sitting at my desk, thinking back on the decades-long journey that led to the creation of *Two Flutes Playing, Two Hearts Dancing,* and now this book, all of which wrote themselves through me. And Churah is standing in spirit right behind my right shoulder. As he leans close and whispers in my right ear, "Darling. This is how to end your book. With a little invocation, incantation." And I start typing:

You who are reading these words—you are holy.

You who are holy, and chose to come back into the world, you are a part of its healing.

You who are a part of the healing of the world, rejoice. For you are the hope of the future.

You and all the men who love men who are our tribe, can unite the world in ways that very few other people can. For we are a people who are defined by our capacity to love. And love is God. And love is what will heal the world.

Now take a deep breath.

And smile.

And feel and see and hear and smell—that you are sitting in a sacred grove of trees, in a grove of trees sacred to our loving tribe of men.

And put your hands on your head and say: "I am wise, I am ancient, I am powerful, I am new. I'm a blessing. I'm a healing. I am needed. I am here."

And put your hands on your heart and say, "I am holy, I am ancient, I am powerful, I am present. I'm a blessing. I'm a healing. I am loving. I am here."

And place your hands on your belly and say: "I am beautiful, I am holy, I am grounded, I am free. I'm a blessing. I'm a healing. I am needed. I am here."

And cup your hands over your genitals and say: "I am grounded, I am holy, I am nurturing, I am wise. I'm a blessing. You're a healing. We have Come In. We are Home."

Now take four long slow breaths, inhaling through your nose and exhaling through your nose. And feel your sacred chosen body, and feel the energy around you, and feel and know that you are not alone, ever. That you are companioned by and traveling with the spirits, the souls, of your and our sacred brothers who are no long embodied. And know and feel that you can feel us. And know that some of you may hear us, that some of us may write or draw and sing or dance with and for and through you. And know that just as this and its companion volumes came through the man whose name is on their covers, that much can come through you too, much that is wanted and needed by the world.

Now take another slow deep breath. And smile. And open. And allow what joyousness wants to flow through you from us—to shine and hum and shimmer in the forest of all of your billions of luminous vibrant soul-chanting cells. As you sit with us, love with us, heal with us, gathered together in our sacred shining grove.

A Beginning

Eli Andrew Ramer

Tuesday June 25th 2024
Oak/land, California
Occupied home of the Ohlone people

Author Bio

PSALM 90 IN THE Bible tells us that we are given seventy years of life, eighty if we're strong. When he turned seventy Andrew Ramer changed his name, and although he still publishes as Andrew, you can call him Eli—for now. If he lives to be eighty he may change his name again. He's considering: Oak.

Eli Andrew Ramer is the author and co-author of several books including the international best seller *Ask Your Angels, Angel Answers, Revelations for a New Millennium,* and five books of queer Jewish stories, *Queering the Text, Torah Told Different, Deathless, Fragments of the Brooklyn Talmud,* and *Texting with Angels*. In *Ever After* he extended the lives of eleven famous Western authors, so that they wrote more and lived happily ever after with someone of the same gender.

Born in 1951 in Elm/hurst, New York, across the street from an amusement park called Fairyland, Eli Ramer now lives in Oak/land, California, up the street from an amusement park called—Fairyland. Ordained a maggid, a sacred storyteller in the Jewish tradition, in 2012, he continues to write, teach, and go for four hour walks, lightly caressing every tree he passes, elm, redwood, palm, maple, eucalyptus, oak . . . . .

Acknowledgments

I WANT TO BEGIN with a great big thank you to Don Shewey, whose remarkable book *Daddy Lover God* inspired this one! I invite you to read it yourself if you haven't already. Thank you Doctor Shewey for all of your amazing writing, for the wonderful things you do to make this a better world, for the blessing of decades of friendship, and for your wonderful foreword to *Two Hearts Dancing*. Don is a noted journalist, psychotherapist, somatic sex educator, and pleasure activist. In addition to *Daddy Lover God: a sacred intimate journey* and *The Paradox of Porn: Notes on Gay Male Sexual Culture*, he has published three books about theater, along with essays in many anthologies and articles in numerous publications including The New York Times, the Village Voice, Esquire, and Rolling Stone. For more information on Don and his work, please visit his website—donshewey.com. I and this book's readers bow to you with gratitude and delight.

Thank you Gordon Binder for the evocative painting on the cover. Gordon, whose art I discovered in the gay/queer magazine *RFD,* is a resident of Washington DC for more than 50 years, during which he enjoyed a long career in the field of environment and conservation. His paintings and drawings feature cityscapes, landscapes, and figurative work, the latter capturing people he sees, mostly men, out and about on the street, in parks and bars and other venues. Gordon is a member of a cooperative gallery in DC (www.studiogallerydc.com) where he serves as the gallery's treasurer. His background and artwork can be seen on his website: www.BinderRawsonArtwork.com, which he shares with his husband Michael Rawson, who is also an artist.

This book opens with the amazing blessing-words of my old friend Toby Johnson. Thank you Toby for wonderfully framing this book as you did and for grounding it in our history in a magically expansive way. Your work has been and continues to be a huge inspiration to so many of us in the gay/queer community down through the years, as a writer yourself and as someone who has supported the work of so many other writers. We all thank you, over and over again! You can learn more about Toby's writings and teachings on gay/queer spirituality at his website— www.tobyjohnson.com.

Thank you Hunter Flournoy for walking with me through the woods as the leaves of this book emerged, once and then once again. And thank you for your amazing capacity to see both the forest *and* the trees. I celebrate you and your luminous work as an editor, life coach, therapist, teacher, writer, and gay tour guide, whose work is grounded in the mystical traditions of the world. And I thank you for all the many blessings of our wonderful friendship. Hunter is the founder and director of Spirit Journeys. For more information on Hunter and his work in the shamanic and mystical traditions, please visit www.spiritjourneys.com and www.hunterflournoy.com

The Sacred Intimate Handbook was dictated to me by the same guides who wrote *Two Flutes Playing*. Thank you all. With great big ongoing thanks to Joseph Kramer who first published *Two Flutes Playing* and invited me to write the handbook. My own copy disappeared some time ago. Thank you to the late Sequoia Lundy and David Hoe for sending me a copy. And read Sequoia's amazing memoir *Divining Desire* about the connection between eroticism and spirituality!

Thanks to The New York Healing Circle, which came together at the height of the AIDS Epidemic. It was there, with the encouragement and support of many including Samuel Kirschner, Nelson Bloncourt, Annie Sprinkle, and the late John Fletcher Harris, that I

ACKNOWLEDGMENTS

began to lead the movement and meditation sessions that became part of our shared work, which spiral out into this book all these decades later. With thanks to you and everyone who sang, danced, chanted, shared, prayed, meditated, and mourned together.

Thanks to The Gay Spirit Visions Conference and all the men I was blessed to be able to journey with, too many to name here, including the late Raven Wolfdancer and King Thackston, whose wonderful art hangs on the walls around me as I type, along with several men who have been an ongoing part of my life for years now, including Don Shewey, Hunter Flournoy, Jonathan Lerner, Andrew Lawler, David-Michael Searcy, and John Myers, all of whom were and are a blessing to me and are among the co-parents of this book.

Thank you to the inner core of my ongoing life-support crew, Jay, Jasminder, Patanjali, Richard, and my regular walking and talking companions, who held me in place as I was working on this book: Steve, Marc, Cheryl, Lyssa, David-Michael, John, Randy, Sheri, Ruth, Avi, Nicki, Niku, Eileen, Cindy, Aysha, Yasser, Patricia, Annalise, Karen, Dev, Sara, Rose-Anne, Carey, Brian, Salem, Michael, Anne, Kate, my spiritual communities, Congregation Sha'ar Zahav, and the First Mennonite Church of San Francisco. Thank you Leo Hill for creating and sustaining my online presence in the world. And to Lake Merritt and all who live in and around it—fish, bat rays, oaks, pines, redwoods, egrets, pelicans, herons, and all the little human who smile up at me from their strollers.

With deep ongoing thanks to the guides and angels who wander the forests of life, guiding me along the trails of meaning with the ZNA that fertilized this book. You are its true authors and I am forever blessed by you and by the chance to share your blessings.

With deep gratitude to the Wipf and Stock team!

Thank you all!

www.ingramcontent.com/pod-product-compliance
Lightning Source LLC
Chambersburg PA
CBHW070442090426
42735CB00012B/2438